The
Central
Motion

W9-BLS-067

Also by James Dickey

Poetry

Into the Stone
Drowning with Others
Helmets
Two Poems of the Air
Buckdancer's Choice
Poems 1957-1967
The Eye-beaters, Blood, Victory,
    Madness, Buckhead and Mercy
The Zodiac
The Strength of Fields
The Early Motion
Falling, May Day Sermon,
    and Other Poems
Puella

Prose

Jericho: The South Beheld
God's Images

Fiction

Deliverance

Children's Poetry

Tucky the Hunter

Criticism

Sorties
The Suspect in Poetry
Babel to Byzantium

Belles-Lettres

Self-Interviews

The
Central
Motion

POEMS,

1968-1979

James Dickey

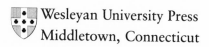 Wesleyan University Press
Middletown, Connecticut

Acknowledgments: This volume is a collection of the poems previously published in the three books *The Eye-Beaters, Blood, Victory, Madness, Buckhead and Mercy*, *The Zodiac*, and *The Strength of Fields*. It is published by arrangement with Doubleday & Company, Inc.

Poems in *The Eye-Beaters* . . . have previously been published as follows: "Sugar," "Under Buzzards," "The Cancer Match," "Venom," "Blood," and the last three sections of "Pine" in *Poetry*, Copyright © 1969 by Modern Poetry Association; "Butterflies," "Giving A Son to the Sea," "The Place," "The Lord in the Air," "Knock," "Madness," and the first two sections of "Pine" appeared originally in *The New Yorker*; "Mercy" and "Looking For The Buckhead Boys" in *The Atlantic Monthly*, Copyright © 1969 by The Atlantic Monthly Company, and "Victory" in *The Atlantic Monthly*, Copyright © 1968 by The Atlantic Monthly Company; "Turning Away" in *Hudson Review*, Copyright © 1966 by The Hudson Review; "The Eye-Beaters and Living There" in *Harper's Magazine*; "For The First Manned Moon Orbit" and "The Moon Ground" in *Life*.

The title poem in *The Strength of Fields* originally appeared in 1977 called *A New Spirit, a New Commitment, a New America*, by the 1977 Inaugural Committee, published by Bantam Books. Copyright © by James Dickey.

"I Dreamed I Already Loved You," "Assignation," and "Doing the Twist on Nails," translated by James Dickey, are all from *Stolen Apples*, by Yevgeny Yevtushenko. Translation copyright © 1971 by Doubleday & Company, Inc. Reprinted by permission of the publisher.

Some of the other poems in this volume appeared originally in the following publications: "False Youth Autumn: Clothes of the Age" (issue of November 1971), "Reunioning Dialogue" (issue of January 1973), and "Exchanges" (issue of September 1970) in *The Atlantic*; "For the Death of Lombardi" in *Esquire*, © 1971 by Esquire, Inc.; "Haunting the Maneuvers," copyright © 1969 by *Harper's Magazine*, reprinted from the January 1970 issue by permission of *Harper's*; "The Voyage of the Needle" (1978 winter issue) in *Gentlemen's Quarterly*; "The Rain Guitar" (January 8, 1972), "Drums Where I Live" (November 26, 1969), "Root-light, or the Lawyer's Daughter" (November 8, 1969), and "Remnant Water" (March 10, 1973) in *The New Yorker*; "Camden Town" in the 1970 spring issue (Vol. 46, No. 2) of *The Virginia Quarterly*.

"Purgation," "The Ax-God: Sea-Pursuit," "Nameless," "Math," "Judas," "Small Song," "Undersea Fragment in Colons," "Mexican Valley," "Low Voice, Out Loud," "Poem," "When," and "A Saying of Farewell" originally appeared in *Head-Deep in Strange Sounds: Free-Flight Improvisations from the unEnglish*, by James Dickey, published by Paleamon Press, Ltd. Copyright © 1979 by James Dickey. Reprinted by permission of the publisher.

All inquiries and permissions requests should be addressed to the Publisher, Wesleyan University Press, 110 Mt. Vernon Street, Middletown, Connecticut 06457

Distributed by Harper & Row Publishers, Keystone Industrial Park, Scranton, Pennsylvania 18512

LIBRARY OF CONGRESS CATALOGING IN PUBLICATION DATA

Dickey, James.
  The Central Motion.
  I. Title.
PS3554.I32A6 1983 811'.54 83-21734
ISBN 0-8195-5091-4
ISBN 0-8195-6088-x (pbk.)

Manufactured in the United States of America
First printing, 1983; second printing, 1984; third printing, 1987

WESLEYAN POETRY

Preface

I am uncertain about the title of this book, but the idea of the poems contained in it being "central" persuaded me, by its double application, to use it. That this work is middleward in time—roughly—is a matter of mathematics; its centrality in my writing life hangs somewhere between 1951, when I began publishing in magazines, and my death-date, which I project—with what fond hope!—as occurring at some time in my eighties, which would place it around the turn of this particular century, if we make it. The other interpretation concerns the centrality of these poems to the whole of my work, and is more difficult to assess. Since I am determined to experiment in future poems, the three books here may show—do show, I feel—a change of subject matter and method, and, together with some failures of taste and understanding, make up my attempts at writing a different kind of poem from the anecdotal narratives of the previous books and lead forward from them toward further, perhaps more extreme, changes. After "Falling," "The Fiend," and "May Day Sermon," I wrote only one more poem in what I call "block format"; this was "The Eye-Beaters," and it may be the best of them. The book in which it appears also marked the beginning of the verbal experimentalism—in "Pine," particularly—that led to the poems of *Puella* and the others after it. In its subject matter the book reflects my involvement with astronomy and space exploration, a continuation of an interest I began as a boy with Edgar Rice Burroughs's Mars and Venus books. The space poems led indirectly to *The Zodiac*; the emphasis on suggestion and connotation to *Puella*.

The Zodiac itself is an effort, partially comic and partially something else I cannot quite name, to walk the line between the authentic transport of poetic creation and the alcohol-induced delusion that it is taking place. The line is thin, and not straight; my Dutch protagonist teeters at times; at times falls. I sought to deal with risks, and take them, and to have my spokesman exemplify the conviction that the poet must go all-out for his vision, his angle, as it presents itself *at that moment*. A good deal of *The Zodiac* is the self-hypnotized yammering and assertiveness of a drunk, but a drunk who would not be able to achieve his occasionally clear and perhaps deep focus on matters of concern to him unless he had had his inhibitions broken down—or through—by the dangerous means he employs, for he insists on nothing less than a personal connection between an exalted and/or intoxicated state, the starry universe, the condition he calls Time, and words. Taking off from Hendrik Marsman's respectable and ambitious poem and re-inventing almost everything in it, I tried to present a number of states of mind in which the cosmos changes, moment to moment in a single consciousness, from a display of miracles to a delusional nightmare—the horrors of delirium tremens—and then back, all changes being parts of its encounter with that hugely mortal beast, the universe, and the smaller, mega-billion-miled Forms, the animals that comprise some of it, in their stark, hinting, and timorous patterns.

The Strength of Fields continues these preoccupations, and adds some new ones. In "Exchanges," commissioned by the Phi Beta Kappa Society of Harvard University, I set out to create a kind of timeless dialogue of poets, between a voice which stands for me and one composed from the poems of Joseph Trumbull Stickney, a contemporary of Henry Adams and George Cabot Lodge, who died of a brain tumor in 1904. Though it was perhaps a fortunate coincidence that Stickney was a Harvard man, I would have picked his work anyway, for I intended its use to constitute a kind of tribute. A line of his is responsible—if any single line could be—for the beginning of my own writing: the words "And all his island shivered into flowers," which I first read on the island of Okinawa in 1945. I felt a new kind of possibility for myself coming out of the words; I remember distinctly the uprush of gratitude to Stickney. The line brings it back, still, together with what I owe it.

The title poem was also commissioned, in this case by President-elect Jimmy Carter. Such an assignment, especially one of this magnitude and publicity, is difficult to imagine, much less to fulfill. It seemed to me that the poem should be clear without being superficial, if I could so decree and manage, and it must resound, if possible, if not so authoritatively as the verse of Mark Van Doren's Dryden, "like a great bronze ring thrown down on marble," at least without tin. What might have been effected by the poem either on the surface or in the subjective existence of the people who heard or read it, I have no way of knowing, but, though history and politics have taken the course they have, I am increasingly gratified that I said what I did at that time, for the hopeful accession of an honorable and caring man.

The poems from other languages were another kind of experiment. I chose them very nearly at random, mainly on spontaneous grabs at what I guessed to be in them, or what I thought I could imagine by means of them. I don't know all the languages; certainly not

Chinese or Hungarian or Norwegian, Finnish or Russian. I know French fairly well, some Spanish and Italian and a little German; the rest were done either with the aid of someone who did know the original languages, or were taken from French versions. So intense was my involvement in the imaginative release that such encounters seem to make possible that the question of "fairness" to the original texts, and their poets, came quickly to seem irrelevant, for a new order of potentiality seemed to show in glimpses: the creation of a third entity that is neither the original poem nor a literal or even an approximate rendering, but comes to exist by means of intuitive and improvisational powers not employed in the original, arriving out of misreadings, substitutions, leaps, absurdities, wrenchings, embarrassments, and standing at last on its own, by virtue of its own characteristics. I would not ordinarily write in the manner of any of these poems, and I am sure the original poets would not under any circumstances have done so. The result is a bastard product, surely, but with luck a bastard having some kind of vitality, some untoward glow; and new, not possible before, or under other conditions, or with any other second sensibility involved. If there is such glow, it is, no matter what, the radiance one hopes for in any poetry, arrived-at no matter how.

—James Dickey
April, 1983

Contents

The Strength of Fields (1979), 97

Head-Deep in Strange Sounds: Free-Flight Improvisations from the unEnglish, 129

The Eye-Beaters,
Blood, Victory,
Madness, Buckhead,
and Mercy

To Lester Mansfield

Diabetes

I
Sugar

One night I thirsted like a prince
Then like a king
Then like an empire   like a world
On fire. I rose and flowed away and fell
Once more to sleep. In an hour I was back
In the kingdom   staggering, my belly going round with self-
Made night-water, wondering what
The hell. Months of having a tongue
Of flame convinced me: I had better not go
On this way. The doctor was young

And nice. He said, I must tell you,
My friend, that it is needles moderation
And exercise. You don't want to look forward
To gangrene and kidney

Failure   boils blindness infection skin trouble falling
Teeth coma and death.
                    O.K.
                              In sleep my mouth went dry
With my answer   and in it burned the sands
Of time with new fury. Sleep could give me no water
But my own. Gangrene in white
Was in my wife's hand at breakfast
Heaped like a mountain. Moderation, moderation,
My friend, and exercise. Each time the barbell
      Rose   each time a foot fell
      Jogging, it counted itself
One death   two death   three death and resurrection
For a little while. Not bad! I always knew it would have to be
                              somewhere around
            The house: the real
            Symbol of Time I could eat

And live with, coming true when I opened my mouth:
True in the coffee and the child's birthday
Cake   helping sickness be fire-
tongued, sleepless and water-
logged   but not bad, sweet sand
Of time, my friend, an everyday—
A livable death at last.

II

Under Buzzards

[for Robert Penn Warren]

Heavy summer. Heavy. Companion, if we climb our mortal bodies
High with great effort, we shall find ourselves
Flying with the life
Of the birds of death. We have come up
Under buzzards   they face us

Slowly   slowly circling   and as we watch them they turn us
Around, and you and I spin
Slowly, slowly rounding
Out the hill. We are level
Exactly on this moment; exactly on the same bird-

plane with those deaths. They are the salvation of our sense
Of glorious movement. Brother, it is right for us to face
Them every which way, and come to ourselves and come
From every direction
There is. Whirl and stand fast!
Whence cometh death, O Lord?
On the downwind, riding fire,

Of Hogback Ridge.
                  But listen: what is dead here?
They are not falling but waiting   but waiting
Riding, and they may know
The rotten, nervous sweetness of my blood.

Somewhere riding the updraft
Of a far forest fire, they sensed the city sugar
The doctors found in time.
My eyes are green as lettuce with my diet,
My weight is down,

One pocket nailed with needles and injections, the other dragging
With sugar cubes to balance me in life
And hold my blood
Level, level. Tell me, black riders, does this do any good?
Tell me what I need to know about my time
In the world. O out of the fiery

Furnace of pine-woods, in the sap-smoke and crownfire of needles,
Say when I'll die. When will the sugar rise boiling
Against me, and my brain be sweetened
to death?
In heavy summer, like this day.
All right! Physicians, witness! I will shoot my veins
Full of insulin. Let the needle burn
In. From your terrible heads
The flight-blood drains   and you are falling back
Back to the body-raising

Fire.
Heavy summer. Heavy. My blood is clear
For a time. Is it too clear? Heat waves are rising
Without birds. But something is gone from me,
Friend. This is too sensible. Really it is better
To know when to die   better for my blood
To stream with the death-wish of birds.
You know, I had just as soon crush
This doomed syringe
Between two mountain rocks, and bury this needle in needles

Of trees. Companion, open that beer.
How the body works   how hard it works
For its medical books is not

Everything: everything is how
Much glory is in it: heavy summer is right.

For a long drink of beer. Red sugar of my eyeballs
Feels them turn blindly
In the fire   rising   turning   turning
Back to Hogback Ridge, and it is all
Delicious, brother: my body is turning   is flashing unbalanced
sweetness everywhere, and I am calling my birds.

Messages

I

Butterflies

Over and around grass banked and packed short and holding back
Water, we have been
Playing, my son, in pure abandon,
And we still are. We play, and play inside our play and play
Inside of that, where butterflies are increasing
The deeper we get
And lake-water ceases to strain. Ah, to play in a great field of light
With your son, both men, both
Young and old! Ah, it was then, Chris,

As now! You lay down on the earth
Dam, and I rambled forth and did not look and found
And found like a blueprint of animal
Life, the whole skeleton of a cow. O son, left
In pure abandon, I sat down inside the bones in the light
Of pine trees, studying the tiny holes
In the head, and where the ants
Could not get through, the nerves had left
Their messages. I sat in the unmoving hearse
Flying, carried by cow-bones in pure
Abandon, back to you. I picked up the head
And inside the nose-place were packets
And whole undealt decks
Of thin bones, like shaved playing cards.
I won the horns. They twisted loose from the forehead
And would not twist back as I gambled and rocked
With the skull in my lap,
The cow not straining to live. In that car I rode
Far off
  and in
    and in
While you were sleeping off the light
Of the world.

And when I came
From the bone dust in pure abandon, I found you lying on the earth
Dam, slanted in the grass that held back
The water, your hands behind your head,
Gazing through your eyelids into the universal
Light, and the butterflies were going

. . . Here

                                    here

         here
         here

                              from here

   madly over

                     to

   here

                                   here.

They went over you   here   and through you
Here   no   yes and tattered apart,
Beat out over water and back
To earth, and over my oldest
Son asleep: their ragged, brave wings

Pulsed on the blue flowers   shook like the inmost
     Play   and blazed all over and around
          Where you slept holding back
     Water without strain.
                         That is all, but like all joy
On earth and water,
                    in bones and in wings and in light,
          It is a gamble. It is play, son, now
     As then. I put the horns beside you in the grass
And turned back to my handsprings and my leaps.

II

Giving a Son to the Sea

Gentle blondness and the moray eel go at the same time
On in my mind as you grow, who fired at me at the age
          Of six, a Christmas toy for child
          Spies: a bullet with a Special Secret
Message Compartment. My hands undid the bullet meant
          For my heart, and it read aloud
          "I love you." That message hits me most
When I watch you swim, that being your only talent.
The sea obsesses you, and your room is full of it:

               Your room is full
          of flippers and snorkels and books
               On spearfishing.
                         O the depths,
My gentle son. Out of that room and into the real
          Wonder and weightless horror
          Of water   into the shifts of vastness
You will probably go, for someone must lead
     Mankind, your father and your sons,
          Down there to live, or we all die
               Of crowding. Many of yóu
               Will die, in the cold roll
Of the bottom currents, and the life lost

9

More totally than anywhere, there in the dark
Of no breath at all.
                              And I must let you go, out of your gentle
                  Childhood into your own man suspended
                        In its body, slowly waving its feet
              Deeper and deeper, while the dark grows, the cold
                    Grows careless, the sun is put
                    Out by the weight of the planet
              As it sinks to the bottom. Maybe you will find us there
                    An agonizing new life, much like the life
Of the drowned, where we will farm eat sleep and bear children
        Who dream of birds.
                                    Switch on your sea-lamp, then,
            And go downward, son, with your only message
            Echoing. Your message to the world, remember,
                    Came to your father
              At Christmas like a bullet. When the great fish roll
                With you, herded deep in the deepest dance,
                When the shark cuts through your invisible
                    Trail, I will send back
              That message, though nothing that lives
                    Underwater will ever receive it.
              That does not matter, my gentle blond
                  Son. That does not matter.

Mercy

Ah, this night   this night mortality wails out
Over Saint Joseph's   this night and every   over Mercy   Mercy
Mercy Manor. Who can be dressed right for the long cry
Who can have his tie knotted to suit the cinder Doctors'
Parking Lot? O yes I'm walking   and we go   I go
In   into a whorehouse
And convent rolled
Into   into something   into the slant streets of slum
Atlanta. I've brought the House Mother
A bottle of gin. She goes for ice
Rattling the kitchen somewhere over   under
The long cry. Fay hasn't come in
Yet; she's scrubbing
For Doctor Evans. Television bulks as the girls pass
In, rising
Up the stairs, and one says to me, What
Say, Good Looking. Something wails like a held-down saint
In Saint Joseph's. The kids, the Mother   the House
Mother says, all act like babies these days. Some of them are, I say
In a low scream. Not all, she says, not all.
You ever been a nurse?
I ask. No; my husband was in wholesale furniture.
Passed away last year of a kidney
Disease; they couldn't do anything for him
At all: he said you go and work
With those girls who've been so good
To me. And here I am, Good
Looking. Fay ought to be
Here in a little while.
The girls that went up are coming
Down, turning the leaves
Of the sign-out book. You waiting for Fay? Yes.
She'll be a little while. O.K.
More ice, to ice-pack
The gin. The last door opens.
It is Fay. This night mortality wails out. Who died,

My love? Whom could you not do anything for? Is that some stranger's
Blood on your thigh? O love I know you by the lysol smell you give
                    Vaseline. Died   died
On the table.
                        She'll just be a minute. These are good girls, the Mother
Says. Fay's a good girl. She's been married; her aunt's
Keeping the kids. I reckon you know that, though. I do,
                    And I say outside
Of time, there must be some way she can strip
Blood off   somebody's blood   strip and comb down and out
            That long dark hair. She's overhead
                    Naked she's streaming
        In the long cry   she has her face in her hands
            In the shower, thinking of children
                Her children in and out
        Of Saint Joseph's   she is drying   my eyes burn
        Like a towel   and perfume and disinfectant battle
            In her armpits   she is stamping
    On the ceiling to get her shoes to fit: Lord, Lord, where are you,
                Fay? O yes, you big cow-bodied
                Love o yes you have changed
                To black   you are in deep
                Dark and your pale face rages
            With fatigue. Mother   Mother   House
                Mother of Mercy
            Manor, you can have the rest
    Of the gin. The cinders of the parking lot are blazing all around
Saint Joseph's; the doctors are leaving. Turn out the light as you go up
            To your husband's furniture, and come
                Here to me, you big
                Bosomed hard handed hard
        Working worker for Life, you. I'll give you something
            Good   something like a long cry
    Out over the ashes of cars   something like a scream through
                                    hundreds of bright
            Bolted-down windows. O take me into
            Your black. Without caring, care
        For me. Hold my head in your wide scrubbed

Hands bring up
My lips. I wail like all
Saint Joseph's   like mortality
This night   and I nearly am dead
In love   Collapsed on the street   struck down
By my heart, with the wail
Coming to me, borne in ambulances voice
By voice into Saint Joseph's   nearly dead
On arrival   on the table beyond
All help: She would bend
Over me like this   sink down
With me in her white dress
Changing to black   we sink
Down flickering
Like television   like Arthur Godfrey's face
Coming on   huge   happy
About us   happy
About everything   O bring up
My lips   hold them down don't let them cry
With the cry   close   closer   eyeball to eyeball
In my arms, O queen of death
Alive, and with me at the end.

Two Poems of Going Home

I
Living There

The Keeper
Is silent   is living in the air not
Breathable, of time. It is gray
Winter in the woods where he lives.
They've been cut down; you can see through
What he is keeping   what used to be a room
In a house with one side turned
To trees. There are no woods now, only other
Houses. Old Self like a younger brother, like a son, we'd come rambling
Out of the house in wagons, turn off the back
Driveway and bump at full bump-speed down
Through the woods, the branches flickering
With us, with the whole thing of home
A blur, gone rolling in leaves. But people are always coming

To know woods   to know rooms in houses
That've been torn down. Where we live, you and I,
My youth and my middle
Age   where we live with our family, miles away
From home, from my old home,
I have rooms
I keep, but this old one, the one where I grew
Up, is in the air
Of winter it is over
Other houses like a ghost. The house lives only
In my head while I look and the sun sinks
Through the floors that were here: the floors
Of time. Brother, it is a long way to the real

House I keep. Those rooms are growing
Intolerable in minds I made
Up, though all seems calm when I walk

Into them as though I belonged there. Sleepers are stirring   an arm lies
Over a face, and the lights are burning
In the fish tank. It is not like this,
But it will be. One day those forms will rise
And leave   and age
And come back   and that house will flame like this
In the Keeper's head
With the last sun; it will be gone,
And someone will not be able
To believe there is only nothing

Where his room was, next to his father's
Blue-eyed   blue-eyed   the fixer   the wagon-master
Blazing in death
With life: will not be able to look
Into windows of the room where he saw,
For the first time, his own blood.
That room fills only with dying
Solar flame   with only the backyard wind
Only the lack
Of trees, of the screech-owl my mother always thought
Was a hurt dog. And tell me for the Lord God
's sake, where are all our old
Dogs?
            Home?
                        Which way is that?
Is it this vacant lot? These woven fences?
Or is it hundreds

Of miles away, where I am the Keeper
Of rooms turning night and day
Into memory? Is it the place I now live
And die in   the place I manage
In? Is it with those people who never knew
These people, except for me? Those people sleeping
Eating my food   loading
Their minds with love   their rooms with what they love
And must lose, and cannot forget? Those fish

Tanks   those James Bond posters   those telescopes
And microscopes and the hidden pictures
Of naked girls? Who are they? And will they come foolishly
Back to stare at nothing
But sunset, where the blood flowed and the wagon wheel grew whole in the
hands
Of the bald-headed father? Will they look into those rooms where now
They sleep, and see nothing but moonlight   nothing but everything
Far and long
Gone, long gone? Why does the Keeper go blind
With sunset? The mad, weeping Keeper who can't keep
A God-damned thing   who knows he can't keep everything
Or anything alive: none of his rooms, his people
His past, his youth, himself,
But cannot let them die? Yes, I keep
Some of those people, not in wagons but in the all-night glimmer
Of fish   in the secret glimmer
Of unfolding girls. I think I know—
I know them well. I call them, for a little while, sons.

II
Looking for the Buckhead Boys

Some of the time, going home, I go
Blind and can't find it.
The house I lived in growing up and out
The doors of high school is torn
Down and cleared
Away for further development, but that does not stop me.
First in the heart
Of my blind spot are
The Buckhead Boys. If I can find them, even one,
I'm home. And if I can find him   catch him in or around
Buckhead, I'll never die: it's likely my youth will walk
Inside me like a king.

First of all, going home, I must go
To Wender and Roberts' Drug Store, for driving through I saw it
Shining   renewed   renewed
In chromium, but still there.
It's one of the places the Buckhead Boys used to be, before
Beer turned teen-ager.
                                        Tommy Nichols
Is not there. The Drug Store is full of women
Made of cosmetics. Tommy Nichols has never been
In such a place: he was the Number Two Man of the Mile
Relay Team in his day.
                                        What day?
My day. Where was I?
                                Number Three, and there are some sunlit pictures
In the Book of the Dead to prove it: the 1939
North Fulton High School Annual. Go down,
                Go down

                To Tyree's Pool Hall, for there was more
                        Concentration of the spirit
                        Of the Buckhead Boys
In there, than anywhere else in the world.
                                                Do I want some shoes
                To walk all over Buckhead like a king
Nobody knows? Well, I can get them at Tyree's;
It's a shoe store now. I could tell you where every spittoon
Ought to be standing. Charlie Gates used to say one of these days
                I'm gonna get myself the reputation of being
The bravest man in Buckhead. I'm going in Tyree's toilet
And pull down my pants and take a shit.
                                                Maybe
Charlie's the key: the man who would say that would never leave
Buckhead. Where is he? Maybe I ought to look up
Some Old Merchants. Why didn't I think of that
                Before?
                Lord, Lord! Like a king!

Hardware. Hardware and Hardware Merchants
Never die, and they have everything on hand
There is to know. Somewhere in the wood-screws Mr. Hamby may have
My Prodigal's Crown on sale. He showed up
For every football game at home
Or away, in the hills of North Georgia. There he is, as old
As ever.
            Mr. Hamby, remember me?
                              God A'Mighty! Ain't you the one
Who fumbled the punt and lost the Russell game?
                                        That's right.
            How're them butter fingers?
                              Still butter, I say,
Still fumbling, But what about the rest of the team? What about Charlie
    Gates?
            He the boy that got lime in his eye from the goal line
When y'all played Gainesville?
                    Right.
                              I don't know. Seems to me I see . . .

See? See? What does Charlie Gates see in his eye burning
With the goal line? Does he see a middle-aged man from the Book
        Of the Dead looking for him in magic shoes
    From Tyree's disappeared pool hall?
                              Mr. Hamby, Mr. Hamby,
    Where? Where is Mont Black?
                        Paralyzed. Doctors can't do nothing.
            Where is Dick Shea?
                        Assistant Sales Manager
Of Kraft Cheese.
            How about Punchy Henderson?
                              Died of a heart attack
            Watching high school football
            In South Carolina.
                        Old Punchy, the last
        Of the windsprinters, and now for no reason the first
            Of the heart attacks.

18

Harmon Quigley?
He's up at County Work Farm
Sixteen. Doing all right up there; be out next year.

Didn't anybody get to be a doctor
Or lawyer?
Sure. Bobby Laster's a chiropractor. He's right out here
At Bolton; got a real good business.
Jack Siple?
Moved away.
Gordon Hamm?
Dead
In the war.

O the Book
Of the Dead, and the dead bright sun on the page
Where the team stands ready to explode
In all directions with Time. Did you say you see Charlie
Gates every now and then?
Seems to me.
Where?
He may be out yonder at the Gulf Station between here and Sandy
Springs.

Let me go pull my car out
Of the parking lot in back
Of Wender and Roberts'. Do I need gas? No; let me drive around the block
Let me drive around Buckhead
A few dozen times   turning   turning in my foreign
Car till the town spins   whirls till the chrome vanishes
From Wender and Roberts'   the spittoons are remade
From the sun itself   the dead pages flutter the hearts rise up, that lie
In the ground, and Bobby Laster's backbreaking fingers
Pick up a cue-stick   Tommy Nichols and I rack the balls
And Charlie Gates walks into Tyree's un-
imaginable toilet.
I go north

Now, and I can use fifty
Cents' worth of gas.
It is Gulf. I pull in and praise the Lord Charlie
Gates comes out. His blue shirt dazzles
Like a baton-pass. He squints he looks at me
Through the goal line. Charlie, Charlie, we have won away from
We have won at home
In the last minute. Can you see me? You say
What I say: where in God
Almighty have you been all this time? I don't know,
Charlie. I don't know. But I've come to tell you a secret
That has to be put into code. Understand what I mean when I say
To the one man who came back alive
From the Book of the Dead   to the bravest man
In Buckhead   to the lime-eyed ghost
Blue-wavering in the fumes
Of good Gulf gas, "Fill 'er up."
With wine? Light? Heart-attack blood? The contents of Tyree's toilet?
The beer
Of teen-age sons? No; just
"Fill 'er up. Fill 'er up, Charlie."

The Place

We are nerve-blowing now. Unspeaking and whiteness around. Warm wind
Was never here. Snow has no move. So this
Has placed us. Dark is with it nearly, for this last of day-
Shaking of shores.

Night is down on us; hold me with all your fur.
These waters have put every grain of their ice
Into our red hand-marrow. Statue-faced, let us breathe
On each other   let us breathe the ice

Sweeping into the air, for it has crossed to
Within us, rigidly airborne, impassable from crossing
Miles of lake-freeze in our
Overwhelming direction. They hang true lovers with thread-

steel through the nose. It hurts straight up and down
Inside us. This is where we come, and we are cross-
eyed with love and every tooth
root aches. Lover, this is where:

I can tell you here.

Apollo

. . . whoever lives out there in space must surely call Earth "the blue planet" . . . ED WHITE

I. *For the First Manned Moon Orbit*

So long
So long as the void
Is hysterical, bolted out, you float on nothing

But procedure alone,

Eating, sleeping like a man
Deprived of the weight of his own
And all humanity in the name

Of a new life
          and through this, making new
Time slowly, the moon comes.
                         Its mountains bulge
    They crack they hold together
    Closer   spreading   smashed crust
Of uncanny rock   ash-glowing   alchemicalizing the sun
    With peace: with the peace of a country
Bombed-out by the universe.
                 You lean back from the great light-
    shattered face   the pale blaze
    Of God-stone coming

    Close   too close, and the dead seas turn
      The craters hover   turn
      Their dark side to kill
      The radio, and the one voice
Of earth.
        You and your computers have brought out
    The silence of mountains the animal
    Eye has not seen since the earth split,

Since God first found geometry
Would move   move
In mysterious ways. You hang

Mysteriously, pulling   the moon-dark pulling,
And solitude breaks down
Like an electrical system: it is something

Else: nothing is something
Something I am trying
To say O God

Almighty! To come back! To complete the curve   to come back
Singing with procedure   back through the last dark
Of the moon, past the dim ritual
Random stones of oblivion, and through the blinding edge
Of moonlight into the sun

And behold

The blue planet steeped in its dream

Of reality, its calculated vision shaking with
The only love.

II. *The Moon Ground*

You look as though
You know me, though the world we came from is striking
You in the forehead like Apollo. Buddy,
We have brought the gods. We know what it is to shine
Far off, with earth. We alone
Of all men, could take off
Our shoes and fly. One-sixth of ourselves, we have gathered,
Both of us, under another one
Of us overhead. He is reading the dials he is understanding
Time, to save our lives. You and I are in earth
light and deep moon
shadow on magic ground
Of the dead new world, and we do not but we could
Leap over each other like children in the universal playground
of stones
but we must not play
At being here: we must look
We must look for it: the stones are going to tell us
Not the why but the how of all things. Brother, your gold face flashes
On me. It is the earth. I hear your deep voice rumbling from the body
Of its huge clothes   Why did we come here

It does not say, but the ground looms, and the secret
Of time is lying
Within amazing reach. It is everywhere
We walk, our glass heads shimmering with absolute heat
And cold. We leap slowly
Along it. We will take back the very stones
Of Time, and build it where we live. Or in the cloud
striped blue of home, will the secret crumble
In our hands with air? Will the moon-plague kill our children
In their beds? The Human Planet trembles in its black
Sky with what we do   I can see it hanging in the god-gold only
Brother of your face. We are this world: we are
The only men. What hope is there at home
In the azure of breath, or here with the stone
Dead secret? My massive clothes bubble around me
Crackling with static and Gray's
Elegy helplessly coming
From my heart, and I say I think something
From high school I remember Now
Fades the glimmering landscape on the sight, and all the air
A solemn stillness holds. Earth glimmers
And in its air-color a solemn stillness holds
It. O brother! Earth-faced god! APOLLO! My eyes blind
With unreachable tears   my breath goes all over
Me and cannot escape. We are here to do one
Thing only, and that is rock by rock to carry the moon to take it
Back. Our clothes embrace we cannot touch we cannot
Kneel. We stare into the moon
dust, the earth-blazing ground. We laugh, with the beautiful craze
Of static. We bend, we pick up stones.

26

The Cancer Match

Lord, you've sent both
And may have come yourself. I will sit down, bearing up under
The death of light very well, and we will all
Have a drink. Two or three, maybe.
I see now the delights

Of being let "come home"
From the hospital.
Night!
I don't have all the time
In the world, but I have all night.
I have space for me and my house,
And I have cancer and whiskey

In a lovely relation.
They are squared off, here on my ground. They are fighting,
Or are they dancing? I have been told   and told
That medicine has no hope, or anything
More to give,

But they have no idea
What hope is, or how it comes, You take these two things:
This bourbon and this thing growing. Why,
They are like boys! They bow
To each other

Like judo masters,
One of them jumping for joy, and I watch them struggle
All around the room, inside and out
Of the house, as they battle
Near the mailbox

And superbly
For the street-lights! Internally, I rise like my old self
To watch: and remember, ladies and gentlemen,

We are looking at this match
From the standpoint

Of tonight
Alone. Swarm over him, my joy, my laughter, my Basic Life
Force! Let your bright sword-arm stream
Into that turgid hulk, the worst
Of me, growing:

Get 'im, O Self
Like a belovèd son! One more time! Tonight we are going
Good   better and better   we are going
To win, and not only win but win
Big, win big.

Venom

[for William Haast]

Forever, it comes from the head. *Where does it end?*
In life-blood. All over it, in fact, like thrown
Off and thrown-again light. There is little help
For it, but there is some.

The priest of poison: where is he? Who is
His latest snake? How does he work?

He has taken it all, brother, and his body lies
With its hand in ice, in a lung

Of iron
                    but at last he rises, his heart changing
What the snake thought. Tooth-marks all over
Him are chattering of life, not death, not
What God gave them. He shimmers

With healing. He will lie down again
With him the snake has entered.
His blood will flow the length
Of the veins of both. They will clasp arms and double-dream

Of the snake in the low long smothering
Sun. Look down! They stretch out giving
And taking. Clouds of family beat the windows
Of doctors with their breath. Here lies

The man made good by a hundred
Bites. It is not God but a human
Body they pray to: Turn the poison
Round turn it back on itself O turn it

Good: better than life they whisper:
Turn it, they hammer whitely:
Turn it, turn it,
Brother.

Blood

In a cold night
Of somebody. Is there other
Breath? What did I say?
Or do?

Mercy.
MERCY!

There is nothing,
But did I do it? I did something.
Merciful, merciful
O God, what? And

Am I still drunk?
Not enough O

Is there any light O where
Do you *touch* this room?
O father

Of Heaven my head cannot
Lift but my hand maybe—
Nobody is breathing   what weapon
Was it? Light smashes

Down there is nothing but
Blood blood all over

Me and blood. Her hair is smeared.
My God what has got loose
In here at last? Who *is*

This girl? She is
Some other town some far
From home: knife

Razor, fingernails O she has been opened
Somewhere and yet

She sighs she turns in the slaughtered sheets
To me in the blood of her children.
Where in what month?

In the cold in the blood
Of life, she turns
to me, and my weapon
will never recover its blood.
Who is

This woman? No matter; she is safe.
She is safe with me.

In the Pocket

NFL

Going backward
All of me and some
Of my friends are forming a shell   my arm is looking
Everywhere and some are breaking
In   breaking down
And out   breaking
Across, and one is going deep   deeper
Than my arm. Where is Number One hooking
Into the violent green alive
With linebackers? I cannot find him he cannot beat
His man   I fall back more
Into the pocket   it is raging and breaking
Number Two has disappeared into the chalk
Of the sideline   Number Three is cutting with half
A step of grace   my friends are crumbling
Around me the wrong color
Is looming   hands are coming
Up and over between
My arm and Number Three: throw it hit him in the middle
Of his enemies   hit move scramble
Before death and the ground
Come up   LEAP STAND KILL DIE STRIKE .

Now.

Knock

Sharing   what sharing   quickly who
Is outside   in   both you together here
And unseen out   let the bed huddle and jump

Naked in the quick dead middle
Of the night, making what is to be
There   you being broken by something

Open where the door thins out
Making frames of the room's early-
warning wood   is the code still

The same can the five fingers
Of the hand still show against
Anything? Have they come for us?

Victory

By September *3rd* I had made my bundle
Of boards and a bag of nails. America, I was high
On Okinawa, with the fleet lying on its back
Under me, whispering "I can't help it"

                                           and all ships firing up fire
Fighting liquids   sucking seawater, hoses climbing and coloring
The air, for Victory. I was clear-seeing
The morning   far-seeing backward
And forward from the cliff. I turned on the ground
And dug in, my nails and bag of magic
Boards from the tent-floor trembling to be
A throne. I was ready to sail
The island toward life
After death, left hand following right into the snail
shelled ground, then knocking down and nailing down my chair like a box
seat in the worldwide window of peace   and sat and lay down my arms
On the stomped grains of ammo-crates heavy with the soles
Of buddies who had helped me wreck the tent
In peace-joy, and of others long buried
At sea. The island rocked with the spectrum
Bombardment of the fleet   and there I was
For sure   saved and plucked naked to my shirt
And lids. I raised my head to the sun.
What I saw was two birthdays

Back, in the jungle, before I sailed high on the rainbow
Waters of victory   before the sun
Of armistice morning burned into my chest
The great V of Allied Conquest. Now it was not here
With the ships sucking up fire
Water and spraying it wild
Through every color, or where, unthreatened, my navel burned
Burned like an entry-wound. Lord, I deepened
Memory, and lay in the light high and wide
Open, murmuring "I can't help it" as I went

South in my mind

                                           Yes Mother

                  there were two fine hands
    Driving the jeep: mine, much better than before, for you had sent
Whiskey. What could I do but make the graveyards soar! O you coming
    Allied Victory, I rambled in the night of two birthdays
          Ago, the battle of Buna stoned
   In moonlight   stone-dead left and right   going nowhere
      Near friend or foe, but turned off into the thickest
  Dark. O yes, Mother, let me tell you: the vines split and locked:
          About where you'd never know me is
          Where I stalled
                       and sat bolt up-
          right in the moonlit bucket
     Seat throne of war
                    cascading the bottle to drink
    To victory, and to what I would do, when the time came,
      With my body. The world leapt like the world
Driving nails, and the moon burned with the light it had when it split

      From the earth. I slept and it was foretold
       That I would live. My head came true
  In a great smile. I reached for the bottle. It was dying and the moon
     Writhed closer to be free; it could answer
My smile of foreknowledge. I forgot the mosquitoes that were going
     Mad on my blood, of biting me once too often on the bites
   Of bites. Had the Form in the moon come from the dead soldier
    Of your bottle, Mother? Let down in blocked
  Out light, a snakehead hung, its eyes putting into mine
Visions of a victory at sea. New Guinea froze. Midair was steady

     Between. Snake-eyes needle-eyed   its
      Lips halving its head
    Stayed shut. I held up the last drop
     In the bottle, and invited him
     To sin   to celebrate

The Allied victory to come. He pulled back a little over
The evil of the thing I meant
To stand for brotherhood. Nightshining his scales on Detroit
Glass, he stayed on and on
My mind. I found out the angel
Of peace is limbless and the day will come
I said, when no difference is between
My skin and the great fleets
Delirious with survival. Mother, I was drunk enough on your birthday
Present, not to die there. I backed the jeep out
Of the Buna weeds
                and, finally, where the sun struck
The side of the hill, there I was
                      back from the dark side
Of the mind, burning like a prism over the conquering Catherine
Wheel of the fleet. But ah, I turned

        I sank I lay back dead
Drunk on a cold table   I had closed my eyes
    And gone north   and lay to change
Colors all night. Out of the Nothing of occupation
Duty, I must have asked for the snake: I asked or the enemy told
Or my snakeskin told
Itself to be. Before I knew it in Yokahama, it was at my throat
Beginning with its tail, cutting through the world
wide Victory sign   moving under
My armpit like a sailor's, scale
By scale. Carbon-arc-light spat in the faces of the four
Men who bent over me, for the future lay brilliantly in
The needles of the enemy. Naked I lay on their zinc
Table, murmuring "I can't help it."
He coiled around me, yet

Headless   I turned with him side
To side, as the peaceful enemy
Designed   a spectrum of scales O yes
Mother I was in the tattoo parlor to this day
Not knowing how I got there as he grew,

Red scales sucking up color   blue
White with my skin running out of the world
Wide sun. Frothing with pinpricks, filling with ink
I lay and it lay
Now over my heart   limbless I fell and moved like moonlight
On the needles   moving to hang my head
In a drunk boy's face, and watch him while he dreamed
Of victory at sea. I retched but choked
It back, for he had crossed my breast, and I knew that many-
colored snakeskin was living with my heart   our hearts
Beat as one   port-of-call red   Yokahoma blue
O yes and now he lay low

On my belly, and gathered together the rainbow
Ships of Buckner Bay. I slumbered deep and he crossed the small
Of my back   increased
His patchwork hold on my hip   passed through the V between
My legs, and came
Around once more   all but the head   then I was turning   the snake
Coiled round my right thigh and crossed
Me with light hands   I felt myself opened
Just enough, where the serpent staggered on his last
Colors   needles gasping for air   jack-hammering
My right haunch burned by the hundreds
Of holes, as the snake shone on me complete   escaping
Forever   surviving   crushing   going home
To the bowels of the living,
His master, and the new prince of peace.

The Lord in the Air

. . . If the spectator could . . . make a
friend & companion of one of these Images
of wonder . . . then would he meet the Lord
in the air & . . . be happy.   BLAKE

Shook down   shook up on these trees they have come
From moment to this moment floating on   in   and this
Moment changes now not with the light for my son
Has come   has come out with one crow floating
Off a limb   back on and off   off a limb in other
Sunlight turning and making him call himself

Blacker   then settles back   back into the other
Moment. They hunch and face in. O yes they are all in
These very trees of the son-faced and fenced-
in backyard   waiting for my boy and the Lord
In the air. O parents great things can be released
From your left-handed son's left hand! They don't know

It, but he has them all in his palm, and now puts them
All in his mouth. Out by the blue swoon of the pool
He lifts the wood whistle to his blond lips. A scratch-
long sound rises out of him   the trees flap and fall
Back, and ah there are crows dealt out all over inside
The light   they mix and mingle   dive   swerve throughout

Themselves   calling   self-shuffling   saying
With my boy's other tongue   sailing   meeting the Lord
Of their stolen voice in the air   and more incoming from miles
Away are here   they wheel in blast after blast
In the child's lungs, as he speaks to them in the only
Word they understand   the *one*   the syllable that means

Everything to them   he has them cold: their several
Accents   they cry with him they know more than all

They have known   fear grief good danger love and marriage
     With the Lord in the air. The pool trembles   my boy falls
       From his voice   falls in stitches to the concrete   one
More word he says   not intended   never heard   he gives

     Them a tone never struck in the egg   in the million years
Of their voice   the whole sky laughs with crows   they creak
   And croak with hilarity   black winged belly-laughs they tell
        Each other   the great joke of flight   sound living
Deep in the sun and waiting   a sound more or less   or more
     Like warning, like marriage. O Chris come in, drop off now

Black birds from your tongue of wood, back into our neighbor
Trees   into other dimensions, their added-to moment and light
Plays over the pool in lovely silence like new   surely like new
     Power over birds and beasts: something that has come in
From all over   come out but not for betrayal, or to call
Up death or desire, but only to give   give what was never.

Pine

successive apprehensions

I

Low-cloudly it whistles, changing heads
On you. How hard to hold and shape head-round.
So any hard hold
Now loses; form breathes near. Close to forest-form
By ear, so landscape is eyelessly
Sighing through needle-eyes. O drawn off
The deep end, step right up
And be where. It could be a net
Spreading field: mid-whistling crossed with an edge and a life
Guarding sound. Overhead assign the bright and dark
Heels distance-running from all   overdrawing the only sound
Of this sound   sound of a life-mass
Drawn in long lines in the air   unbroken   brother-saving
Sound merely soft
And loudly soft just in time   then nothing and then
Soft   soft and a little caring-for   sift-softening
And soared-to. O ankle-wings lightening and fleeing
Brothers sending back for you
To join the air and live right: O justice-scales leaning toward mercy
Wherever. Justice is exciting in the wind
As escape continuing   as an ax hurling
Toward sound and shock. Nothing so just as wind
In its place in low cloud
Of its tree-voice stopped and on-going   footless flight
Sound like brothers coming on as
All-comers coming and fleeing
From ear-you and pine, and all pine.

II

What mainly for the brow-hair
Has been blowing, dimensions and glows in:

40

Air the most like
Transfusion expands and only
There it is fresh
From overhead, steep-brewing and heavy from deep
Down upcoming new
To the lungs like a lean cave swimming—
Throat-light and iron
Warm spray on the inside face
Cutting often and cooling-out and brow
Opening and haunting freshly. So have you changed to this
You like a sea-wall
Tarred as a stump and blowing
Your skull like clover   lung-swimming in rosin
Dwelling
        by breath
              breath:
Whose head like a cave opens living
With eddies   needle-sapped out
Of its mind by this face-lifting
Face like a tree-beast
Listening, resetting the man-broken nose
bones on wine
Currents, as taste goes wild
And wells up   recalls   recovers and calls
For its own, for pure spirit
Food: windfalls and wavers out again
From nothing, in green sinus-packs.

III

More and more, through slow breaks
In the wind   no a different no this
Wind, another life of you rises,
A saliva-gland burns like a tree.
You are what you eat
           and what will flutter
Like food if you turn completely
To your mouth, and stand wide open?

A wafer of bark, another
Needle, bitter rain by the mouthful coming.
Hunger swirls and slowly down
Showers   and are your children
What you eat? What green of horror
And manna in the next eye
To come from you? And will he whistle
From head to foot?

Bitter rain by the mouthful coming.

IV

More hands on the terrible rough.
More pain but more than all
Is lodged in the leg-insides. More holding,
Though, more swaying. Rise and ride
Like this and wear and ride
Away with a passionate faceful
Of ply and points. The whole thing turns
On earth, throwing off a dark
Flood of four ways
Of being here blind and bending
Blacked-out and framed
Suspended and found alive in the rough palm-
And thigh-fires of friction, embracing in the beyond
It all, where,
Opening one by one, you still can open
One thing more. A final form
And color at last comes out
Of you alone putting it all
Together like nothing
Here like almighty

V

Glory.

Madness

(Time: Spring. Place: Virginia. A
domestic dog wanders from the house,
is bitten by a rabid female fox, runs
mad himself, and has to be hunted
down, killed, and beheaded.)

Lay in the house mostly living
With children when they called   mostly
Under the table begging for scraps lay with the head
On a family foot
Or stretched out on a side,
Firesided. Had no running
Running, ever.
Would lie relaxed, eyes dim

With appreciation, licking the pure contentment
Of long   long notched
Black lips. Would lap up milk like a cat and swim clear
In brown grateful eyes. That was then, before the Spring
Lay down and out
Under a tree, not far but a little far and out
Of sight of the house.
Rain had sown thick and gone

From the house where the living
Was done, where scraps fell and fire banked full
On one sleeping side of the spirit
Of the household
                    and it was best
To get up and wander
Out, out of sight. Help me was shouted
To the world of females   anyone will do
To the smoking leaves.

Love could be smelt. All things burned deep
In eyes that were dim from looking
At the undersides of tables   patient with being the god
Of small children. In Spring it is better with no
Doors which the god
Of households must beg at   no locks where the winds blows
The world's furry women
About in heat. And there

She lay, firesided, bushy-assed, her head
On the ground wide open, slopping soap:
Come   come close
She said like a god's
Wild mistress said come
On boy, I'm what you come

Out here in the bushes for. She burned alive
In her smell, and the eyes she looked at burned
With gratitude, thrown a point-eared scrap
Of the world's women, hot-tailed and hunted: she bit down
Hard on a great yell
To the house being eaten alive
By April's leaves. Bawled; they came and found.
The children cried

Helping tote to the full moon
Of the kitchen   "I carried the head"   O full of eyes
Heads kept coming across, and friends and family
Hurt   hurt
The spirit of the household, on the kitchen
Table being thick-sewed   they saying it was barbed
Wire looked like
It got him, and he had no business running

Off like that. Black lips curled as they bathed off
Blood, bathed blood. Staggered up under
The table making loud
A low-born sound, and went feeling

For the outer limits
Of the woods   felt them break and take in
The world   the frame turn loose and the house
Not mean what it said it was. Lay down and out
Of sight and could not get up
The head, lying on God's foot firesided
Fireheaded   formed a thought
Of Spring   of trees in wildfire
Of the mind speeded up   and put all thirst

Into the leaves. They grew
Unlimited. Soap boiled
Between black lips: the house
Spirit jumped up beyond   began to run   shot
Through the yard and bit down
On the youngest child. And when it sprang down
And out across the pasture, the grains of its footprints leapt
Free, where horses that shied from its low

New sound were gathered, and men swung themselves
Up to learn what Spring
Had a new way to tell, by bringing up
And out the speed of the fields. A long horn blew
Firesided   the mad head sang
Along the furrows   bouncing and echoing from earth
To earth through the body
Turning   doubling back
Through the weather of love running wild and the horses full

Of strangers coming after. Fence wire fell and rose
Flaming with messages as the spirit ran
Ran with house-hair
Burr-picking madly   and after came

Men   horses   spirits
Of households leaping crazily beyond
Their limits, dragging their bodies by the foaming throat through grass
And beggar-lice and by the red dust

Road where men blazed and roared
With their shoulders   blew it down and apart where it ran
And lay down on the earth of God's
One foot and the foot beneath the table kicked
The white mouth shut: this was something

In Spring in mild brown eyes   as strangers
Cut off the head and carried and held it
Up, blazing with consequence   blazing
With freedom saying   bringing
Help   help   madness   help.

The Eye-Beaters

[for Mary Bookwalter]

*A man visits
a Home for chil-
dren in Indiana,
some of whom
have gone blind
there.*

Come something   come blood sunlight   come and they break
Through the child-wall, taking heart from the two left feet
Of your sound: are groping for the Visitor in the tall corn
Green of Indiana. You may be the light, for they have seen it
                                              coming
From people: have seen it on cricket and brick have seen it
Seen it fade   seen slowly the edge of things fail   all corn
Green fail   heard fields grind   press with insects and go round
To the back of the head. They are blind. Listen   listen well

*A therapist
explains why
the children
strike
their eyes.*

To your walking that gathers the blind in bonds   gathers these
Who have fought with themselves   have blacked their eyes wide
Open, toddling like dolls and like penguins   soft-knotted down,
Protected, arms bound to their sides in gauze, but dark is not
To be stood in that way: they holler   howl till they can shred
Their gentle ropes   whirl and come loose. They *know* they
                                              should see
But *what*, now? When their fists smash their eyeballs, they behold
                                                   no
Stranger giving light from his palms. What they glimpse has flared
In mankind from the beginning. In the asylum, children turn to
                                              go back
Into the race: turn their heads without comment into the black
                                              magic
Migraine of caves. Smudge-eyed, wide-eyed, gouged, horned, caved-
in, they are silent: it is for you to guess what they hold back inside
The brown and hazel   inside the failed green   the vacant
                                              blue-

*The Visitor
begins to
invent a
fiction to
save his mind.*

eyed floating of the soul. Was that lightning   was that a heart-
struck leap   somewhere before birth? Why do you eat the green
                                              summer
Air like smoky meat? Ah, Stranger, you do not visit this place,
You live or die in it   you brain-scream you beat your eyes to
                                                   see
The junebug take off backwards   spin   connect his body-sound

47

To what he is in the air. But under the fist, on the hand-stomped
                                                                bone,
A bison leaps out of rock   fades   a long-haired nine-year-old
                                                                clubs
Her eye, imploding with vision   dark   bright again   again
                                                                again
A beast, before her arms are tied. Can it be? Lord, when they slug
Their blue cheeks blacker, can it be that they do not see the wings
And green of insects   or the therapist suffering kindly   but
                                                a tribal light old

*He tries to see
what they see
when they beat
their eyes.*

Enough to be seen without sight? There, quiet children stand
                                                watching
A man striped and heavy with pigment, lift his hand with color
                                                coming
From him. Bestial, working like God, he moves on stone he is
                                                drawing
A half-cloud of beasts on the wall. They crane closer, helping,
                                                beating
Harder, light blazing inward from their fists   and see   see
                                                leap
From the shocked head-nerves, great herds of deer on the hacked
                                                glory plain
Of the cave wall: antelope   elk: blind children strike for the
                                                middle
Of the brain, where the race is young. Stranger, they stand here
And fill your mind with beasts: ibex   quagga   rhinoceros of
                                                wool-
gathering smoke: cave bear   aurochs   mammoth: beings
                                                that appear
Only in the memory of caves   the niches filled, not with
                                                Virgins,
But with the squat shapes of the Mother. In glimmers of mid-
                                                brain pain
The forms of animals are struck like water from the stone   where
                                                hunger
And rage   where the Visitor's helplessness and terror   all
Move on the walls and create.

48

(Look up: the sun is taking its stand on four
o'clock of Indiana time, painfully blazing   fist of a ball of fire
God struck from His one eye).
                                              No; you see only dead beasts playing
In the bloody handprint on the stone where God gropes like a
                                                              man
Like a child, for animals   where the artist hunts and slashes,
                                                              glowing
Like entrail-blood, tracking the wounded game across the limestone
As it is conceived. The spoor leads   his hand changes   grows
Hair like a bison   horns like an elk   unshapes   in a deer-
                                                      leap emerges
From the spear-pitted rock, becoming what it can make
                                                          unrolling
Not sparing itself clenching re-forming rising   beating
For light.
                              Ah, you think it, Stranger: you'd like that you try hard
To think it, to think for them. But what you see, in the half-
                                                          inner sight
Of squinting, are only fields   only children whose hands are tied
                                                                  away
From them for their own good   children waiting to smash
                                                      their dead
Eyes, live faces, to see nothing. As before, they come to you smiling,
Using their strange body-English. *But why is it* this *they have*
                                                          made up
In your mind? Why painting and Hunting? Why animals showing
                                                          how God
Is subject to the pictures in the cave   their clotted colors
                                                      like blood
On His hands as the wild horse burns   as the running buck
                                                          turns red
From His palm, while children twist in their white ropes, eyes
                                                              wide,
Their heads in the dark meat of bruises?
                                          And now, blind hunters,
Swaying in concert like corn   sweet-faced   tribe-swaying at
                                                      the red wall

*His Reason
argues with his
invention.*

Of the blind like a cooking-fire   shoulder-moving, moaning as the
                                                                    cave-
artist moaned when he drew the bull-elk to the heart   come
                                                                    ring
Me round. I will undo you. Come, and your hands will be free to fly
Straight into your faces, and shake the human vision to its roots
Flint-chipping sparks spring up: I can see   feel   see
                                        another elk
Ignite with his own becoming: it is time.
                                        Yes, indeed I know it is not
So   I am trying to make it   make something   make them
                                                        make me
Re-invent the vision of the race   knowing the blind must see
By magic or nothing. Therapists, I admit it; it helps me to think
That they can give themselves, like God from their scabby fists,
                                                        the original
Images of mankind: that when they beat their eyes, I witness
                                                        how
I survive, in my sun-blinded mind: that the beasts are calling to
                                                        God
And man for art, when the blind open wide and strike their incurable
                                                                    eyes
In Indiana. *And yet, O Stranger, those beasts and mother-*
                                                figures are all
Made up by you. They are your therapy. There is nothing inside
                                                their dark,
Nothing behind their eyes but the nerve that kills the sun above
                                                the corn
Field   no hunt no meat no pain-struck spark no vision   no
                                                pre-history
For the blind   nothing but blackness forever   nothing but
                                                a new bruise
Risen upon the old.
                        They have gone away; the doors have shut
                                                shut on you
And your makeshift salvation. Yet your head still keeps what you
                                                would put in theirs
If you were God. Bring down your lids like a cave, and try to see

*The children
retire, but he
hears them
behind
their wall.*

50

By the race alone. Collective memory stirs   herd-breathes
                       stamps
In snow-smoke, as the cave takes hold. You are artist and beast and
The picture of the beast: you are a ring of men and the
                  stampeded bones
Tumbling into the meat-pit. A child screams out in fury, but
                     where,
In the time of man? O brother, quiver and sweat: It is true that
                   no thing
Anyone can do is good enough for them: not Braille not data
Processing   not "learning TV repair" not music   no, and
                  not not being
"A burden": none of these, but only vision: what they see must
                  be crucial

He accepts his fiction.   To the human race. It is so; to let you live with yourself after seeing
Them, they must be thought to see by what has caused   is
                  causing us all
To survive. In the late sun of the asylum, you know nothing else
                  will do
You; the rest is mere light. In the palm of the hand the color red
                  is calling
For blood   the forest-fire roars on the cook-stone, smoke-
                  smothered and lightning-
born   and the race hangs on meat and illusion   hangs on
                  nothing
But a magical art. Stranger, you may as well take your own life
Blood   brain-blood, as vision. Yes; that hammering on the
                  door is not
Your heart, or the great pulse of insects; it is blind children
                  beating
Their eyes to throw a picture on the wall. Once more you hear
                  a child yell
In pure killing fury   pure triumph pure acceptance   as
                  his hands burst
Their bonds. It is happening. Half-broken light flickers with agony
Like a head   throwing up the beast-paint the wall cannot
                  shake
For a million years.

Hold on to your fantasy; it is all that can save
A man with good eyes in this place. Hold on, though doctors
                                          keep telling
You to back off   to be what you came as   back off from
                                          the actual
Wall of their screaming room, as green comes all around you with
                                          its ears
Of corn, its local, all-insect hum, given junebugs and flies
                                          wherever
They are, in midair. No;
                    by God. There is no help for this but madness,
Perversity. Think that somewhere under their pummeled lids
                                          they gather
At the wall of art-crazed beasts, and the sun blazing into the
                                          blackout
Of the cave, dies of vision. A spell sways in. It is time for the night
Hunt, and the wild meat of survival. The wall glimmers that God
                                          and man
Never forgot. I have put history out. An innocent eye, it is closed
Off, outside in the sun. Wind moans like an artist. The tribal
                                          children lie
On their rocks in their animal skins   seeing in spurts of
                                          eye-beating
Dream, the deer, still wet with creation, open its image to the heart's

He leaves
the Home.

Blood, as I step forward, as I move through the beast-paint of
                                          the stone,
Taken over, submitting, brain-weeping. Light me a torch with
                                          what we have preserved
Of lightning. Cloud bellows in my hand. God man hunter artist
                                          father
Be with me. My prey is rock-trembling, calling. Beast, get in
My way. Your body opens onto the plain. Deer, take me into
                                          your life-
lined form. I merge, I pass beyond in secret   in perversity and the
                                          sheer
Despair of invention   my double-clear bifocals off   my
                                          reason gone
Like eyes. Therapist, farewell at the living end. Give me my spear.

52

Turning Away

Variations on Estrangement

I

Something for a long time has gone wrong,
Got in between this you and that one other
And now   here   you must turn away.

Beyond! Beyond! Another life moves

In numbing clarity begins
By looking out the simple-minded window,
The face untimely relieved
Of living the expression of its love.

II

Shy, sad, adolescent   separated-out
The gaze stands alone in the meadow
Like a king starting out on a journey
Away from all things that he knows.
It stands there   there

With the ghost's will to see and not tell
What it sees with its nerveless vision
Of sorrow, its queen-killing glare:
The apple tree in the wind
Paling with noon sleep,
Light pouring down from the day-moon
White-hot inside the sun's mildness,

The eyes clamped by an ordinary meadow
As by the latest masterpiece
Under the sun.

III

For the face a studded look slowly
Arrives from a gulley of chickweed
Like a beard, come from something
Unwanted, that the face cannot help all its life.
Hair curls inside the jaws
Unstoppable   mindless   turns white
Turns straight   chokes
Helplessly, in more and more dangerous
Iron-masked silence.

IV

A deadly, dramatic compression
Is made of the normal brow. Because of it
The presence of the hand upon the sill
Calms and does not shake the thing beheld.
Every stone within sight stands ready
To give you its secret
Of impassivity, its unquestionable
Silence: you wear
Its reason for existence where you stand

So still   the tongue grows solid also
Holding back the rock speech.

V

A hooked shape threads
Through your nostrils, and you have
Caesar's eagle look, and nothing
For it to do,
Even though, on the golden

Imperial helmet, little doors close over
Your face, and your head is covered
With military flowers.

VI

Turning away,
You foresee the same fields you watch.
They are there an instant
Before they are ready: a stream being slowly suspended
Between its weeds, running where it once was,
Keeping its choir-sounds going
All like crowned boys
But now among grasses that are
An enormous green bright growing No
That frees forever.

VII

The mutual scar on the hand of man
And woman, earned in the kitchen,
Comes forth   rises for you to brush
Off like a cutworm
As the weed with wings explodes
In air, laying in front of you down
Cheap flowers by hundreds of thousands
And you try to get by heart
The words written after the end

Of every marriage manual, back
To the beginning, saying
Change; form again; flee.

VIII

Despair and exultation
Lie down together and thrash
In the hot grass, no blade moving,
A stark freedom primes your new loins:
Turning away, you can breed
With the farthest women

And the farthest also in time: breed
Through bees, like flowers and bushes:
Breed Greeks, Egyptians and Romans   hoplites
Peasants   caged kings   clairvoyant bastards:
The earth's whole history blazes
To become this light
For you are released to all others,

All places and times of all women,
And for their children hunger
Also: for those who could be half
You, half someone unmet,
Someone dead, immortal, or coming.

Near you, some being suddenly
Also free, is weeping her body away.

IX

The watched fields shake   shake
Half blind with scrutiny.
All working together, grasshoppers
Push on a stem apiece
And the breathless meadow begins
To sway   dissolve   revolve:

Faintness   but the brain rights
Itself with a sigh in the skull

And sees again nothing
But intensified grass. Listen:
When this much is wrong, one can fix one's head

In peacetime   turning away
From an old peaceful love
To a helmet of silent war
Against the universe   and see
What to do with it all: see with the eyes
Of a very great general
Roads ditches trees
Which have sunk their roots to provide
Not shade but covering-fire.

X

Somewhere in this guarded encampment
The soul stands stealthily up
To desert: stands up like the sex
About to run   running
Through pinewoods   creeks   changes of light   night
And day   the wide universe streaming over it
As it stands there panting   over-sensitized
Filled with blood from the feet

Heartbeating   surviving   in the last

Place   in cloud river meadowgrass or grave   waiting
For bird beast or plant to tell it
How to use itself   whom to meet   what to do
Which way to go to join
The most ineffectual army   the defiant, trembling
Corps of the unattached.

XI

Fear passes
Into sweat hidden openly
In the instant new lines of the brow. The field
Deepens in peace, as though, even
Before battle, it were rich-
ening with a generation's
Thousand best, quietest men
In long grass bending east
To west. Turning away, seeing fearful
Ordinary ground, boys' eyes manlike go,
The middle-aged man's like a desperate
Boy's, the old man's like a new angel's

Beholding the river in all
White places   rushing
At and burning its boulders
Quietly   the current laid
In threads   as, idly, a conqueror's horse,

Ox-headed, is born of the shape of a cloud
That was an unnoticed
Deep-hanging bed.
Water waves in the air,
A slant, branded darkness
From a distant field full of horses
Uprisen into a cloud
That is their oversoul.

XII

Under the great drifting stallion
With his foreleg bloatedly cocked, the armed
Men who could spring from your teeth
Double their strength in your jaws:

XIII

So many battles
Fought in cow pastures   fought back
And forth over anybody's farm
With men or only
With wounded eyes—
Fought in the near yellow crops
And the same crops blue farther off.

XIV

Dead armies' breath like a sunflower
Stirs, where the loved-too-long
Lie with a whimper of scythes.
Coming to them, the seeds
Of distant plants either die
Or burn out when they touch
Ground, or are born in this place.
Rain is born rain: let tons of repossessed
Water walk to us!

XV

You may have swallowed a thistle
Or the first drop of rain;
You have been open-mouthed.
Now speak of battles that bring

To light no blood, but strew the meadows
With inner lives:
Speak now with the thistle's sharpness
Piercing   floating   descending
In flowers all over the field
With a dog-noise low in the calyx.

XVI

Like a hound, you can smell the earth change
As your cloud comes over the sun
Like a called horse.
The long field summons its armies
From every underground
Direction. Prepare to fight
The past   flee   lie down,
Heartbeat a noise in your head
Like knocking the rungs from a ladder:
So many things stand wide
Open! Distance is helplessly deep
On all sides   and you can enter, alone,
Anything   anything can go
On wherever it wishes   anywhere in the world or in time
But here and now.

XVII

Turning away, the eyes do not mist over
Despite the alien sobbing in the room.
Withhold! Withhold! Stand by this window
As on guard
Duty   rehearsing what you will answer
If questioned   stand

General   deserter   freed slave belovèd of all,
Giving off behind your back
Ridiculous energy   stand

Like a proof of character learned
From Caesar's *Wars*   from novels
Read in the dark,
Thinking of your life as a thing
That can be learned,
As those earnest young heroes learned theirs,
Later, much later on.

This poem is based on another of the same title.
   It was written by Hendrik Marsman, who was killed
      by a torpedo in the North Atlantic in 1940.
It is in no sense a translation, for the liberties
   I have taken with Marsman's original poem are such
that the poem I publish here,
   with the exception
      of a few lines,
   is completely my own.
Its twelve sections are the story of a drunken
   and perhaps dying Dutch poet who returns to his
      home in Amsterdam after years of travel and
tries desperately to relate himself, by means of stars,
      to the universe.

—homage to Hendrik Marsman, lost at sea, 1940—

The Zodiac

The Man I'm telling you about brought himself back alive
A couple of years ago.   He's here,
    Making no trouble
                        over the broker's peaceful
    Open-bay office at the corner of two canals
        That square off and starfish into four streets
            Stumbling like mine-tunnels all over town.

To the right, his window leaps and blinds
                            and sees
The bridges shrivel on contact with low cloud
                            leaning to reach out
    Of his rent-range
                and get to feudal doors:
        Big-rich houses whose thick basement-stones
            Turn water into cement inch by inch
            As the tide grovels down.
                            When that tide turns
    Hé turns left   his eyes back-swivel into his head
        In hangover-pain like the flu   the flu
            Dizzy with tree-tops
                        all dead, but the eye going
    Barely getting   but getting you're damn right but still
        Getting them.
                        Trees, all right.   No leaves.   All right,

    Trees, stand
                and deliver.   They stand and deliver
    Not much: stand
    Wobble-rooted, in the crumbling docks.
                            So what?

The town square below, deserted as a Siberian crater, lies in the middle
Of his white-writing darkness   stroboscoped   red-stopped by the stammering mess
    Of the city's unbombed neon, sent through rivers and many cities
                By fourth-class mail from Hell.

All right, since you want to, look:

Somebody's lugged a priest's failed prison-cell
Swaybacked up the broker's cut-rate stairs.   He rents it on credit.

No picture
            nothing but a bed and desk
      And empty paper.
                  A flower couldn't make it in this place.
      It couldn't live, or couldn't get here at all.
                  No flower could get up these steps,
                  It'd wither at the hollowness
Of these foot-stomping
                  failed creative-man's boards—
            There's nothing to bring love or death

            Or creative boredom through the walls.
                                          Walls,

            Ah walls.   They're the whole place.   And any time,
      The easting and westing city in the windows
      Plainly are not true
                        without a drink.   But the *walls*—
            Weightless   ridiculous   bare
            Are there just enough to be dreadful
Whether they're spinning or not.   They're there to go round him

      And keep the floor turning with the earth.
He moves among stars.
                  Sure.   We all do, but he is star-*crazed*, mad

   With *Einfühlung*, with connecting and joining things that lay their meanings

            Over billions of light years
                              eons of time—Ah,

            Years of light: billions of them: they are pictures

            Of some sort of meaning.   He thinks the secret

64

Can be read.   But human faces swim through
Cancer   Scorpio   Leo   through all the stupefying design,

And all he can add to it or make of it, living or dead:
An eye lash-flicker, a responsive
light-year light
From the pit of the stomach, and a young face comes on,
Trying for the pit of his poem
strange   remembered
Comes on faintly, like the faint, structural light
Of Alnilam, without which Orion

Would have no center   the Hunter
Could not hunt, in the winter clouds.
The face comes on

Glowing with billions of miles   burning like nebulae,
Like the horse-head nebula in Orion—

She was always a little horse-faced,
At least in profile   she is some strange tint
Of second-order blue: intensity   she is eternal
As long as *he* lives—the stars and his balls meet
And she shows herself as any face does
That *is* eternal, raying in and out
Of the body of a man: in profile   sketched-in by stars
Better than the ones God set turning

Around us forever.
The trees night-pale

Out.   Vacuum.
Absolute living-space-white.   Only one way beyond

The room.
The Zodiac.
He must solve it   must believe it   learn to read it

No, wallow in it

As poetry.

He's drunk.   Other drunks, it's alligators
Or rats, their scales and eyes
Turning the cold moon molten on the floor.—   With him, it's his part-time army

Of soldier ants; they march over
His writing hand, heading for the Amazon Basin.
He can take *them* . . .

He bristles   itches like a sawdust-pile

But something's more important than flesh-crawling
To gain an image
line by line: they give him an idea.   Suppose—

Well, let's just suppose I . . .

No ants.   No idea.   Maybe they'll come back
All wildly drunk, and dance
Into the writing.   It's worth a try.

Hot damn, here they come!   He knows them, name for name
As they surround his fingers, and carry the maze
Onto the paper: they're named for generals.

He thinks
That way: of history, with his skin
with everything

He has, including delirium tremens
staring straight

Into the lamp.   You are a strange creature,

Light,
he says to light.   Maybe one day I'll get something
Bigger than ants   maybe something from the sea.

Keep knocking back the *aquavit*. By the way, my man, get that *aqua!*
There's a time acoming when the life of the sea   when

          The stars and their creatures get together.

Light
          is another way. This is when the sun drifts in
          Like it does in any window, but this sun is coming
From the east part of town.   Shit, I don't know where I am
          This desk is rolling like the sea
                              Come home   come to my home—

I'll never make it to land.   I am alone:
                              I am my brother:

               I look at my own decoration
                         Outside of the page:
                                   three rods: they're turning modernly—

   A mobile he's got up
Above the bed, from splintered bottle-bits and coat-hangers:

   You know they are, there really *are*
               Small, smashed greens revolving
In a room.
               It all hangs together, and *you* made it:
               Its axis is spinning
Through the Zodiac.
                         He flicks it and sets the model
               For a universe of green, see-through stars
Going faster.   The white walls stagger
          With lights:
He has to hold onto the chair: the room is pitching and rolling—
               He's sick   seasick with his own stars,
                         seasick and airsick   sick

With the Zodiac.
               Even drunk

Even in the white, whiskey-struck, splintered star of a bottle-room dancing,
He knows he's not fooling himself   he knows

Not a damn thing of stars   of God   of space

Of time   love night death sex fire numbers signs words,

Not much of poetry.   But by God, we've got a *universe*

Here

Those designs of time are saying *some*thing
Or maybe something or *other*.

Night—

Night tells us.   It's coming—

Venus shades it and breaks it.   Will the animals come back
Gently, creatively open,

Like they were?

Yes.

The great, burning Beings   melt into place
A few billion-lighted inept beasts

Of God—

What else is there?   What other signs   what other symbols

Are *any*thing beside these?   If the thing hasn't been said
This way,   then God can't say it.

Unknown.   Unknown.
His mobile made of human shattering-art

Is idling through space, and also oddly, indifferently,
Supremely, through beauty as well.   Yes,

      Sideways through beauty.   He swirls in his man-made universe,

His room, his liquor, both the new bottle and the old
      Fragmented godlike one.
He never gets tired.   Through his green, moving speckles,

He looks sideways, out and up   and there it is:
      The perpetual Eden of space
                    there when you want it.

What animal's getting outlined?
          All space is being bolted
     Together: eternal blackness

                    studded with creatures.
   Stars.
         Beasts.   Nothing left but the void
            Deep-hammering its creatures with light-years.
   Years made of light.
              Only light.

                 Yes.

    But what about the damned *room?*
God-beast-stars   wine-bottle constellations   jack-off dreams
    And silence. That's about it.

            They're all one-eyed—
The Lion   the Scorpion   the others coming—
    Their one-eyed eyesight billions of years
In the making, making and mixing with his liquor-bottle green
Splintered shadows   *art*-shadows, for God's sake:

    Look, stupid, get your nose out of the sky for once.
There're things that are *close* to you, too. Look at *them!*

Don't cringe: look right out over town.
Real birds. There they are in their curves, moving in their great element
                    That causes our planet to be blue and causes us all
                        To breathe.   Ah, long ghostly drift
            Of wings.
                            Well, son of a bitch.
                                        He sits and writes,
                And the paper begins to run
                                with signs.
                        But he can't get rid of himself enough
        To write poetry.   He keeps thinking Goddamn
            I've misused myself   I've fucked up   I haven't worked—

I've traveled and screwed too much,
                                but   but by dawn, now   NOW
            Something   coming   through-coming   down-coming   up
To me   ME!
                His hand reaches, dazzling with drink   half alive,
            for the half-dead vision.   That room and its page come in and
                                                    out
Of being.   You talk about *looking:*   would you look at *that*
Electric page!   What the hell did I say?   Did *I* say that?
            You bastard, you. Why didn't you know that before?
            Where the hell have you been with your *head?*
You and the paper should have known it, you and the ink: you write

            Everybody writes

With blackness. Night. Why has it taken you all this time?
                    All this travel, all those lives
                You've fucked up? All those books read
        Not deep enough? It's staring you right in the face   The
                                                secret—

    Is whiteness.   You can do *anything* with that.   But no—
        The secret is that on whiteness you can release
        The blackness,
                    the night sky.   Whiteness is death   is dying

For human words to raise it from purity   from the grave
        Of too much light.   Words must come to it
    Words from *any*where   from   from
Swamps   mountains   mud   shit   hospitals   wars   travels   from

        Stars

From the Zodiac.
                You son of a bitch, you! Don't try to get away from yourself!
I won't have it! You know God-damned well I mean you! And you too,
        Pythagoras!   Put down that guitar, lyre, whatever it is!
You've driven me nuts enough with your music of the spheres!
        But I'll bet you know what to know:

    Where God once stood in the stadium
  Of European history, and battled mankind in the blue air
    Of manmade curses, under the exploding flags
Of dawn,   I'd put something else now:
    I'd put something overhead   something new: a new beast

For the Zodiac.   I'd say to myself like a man

            Bartending for God,
                    What'll it be?
Great! The stars are mine, and so is
                The imagination to work them—
                            To create.
        Christ, would you tell me why my head
Keeps thinking up these nit-witted, useless images?

            Whiskey helps.
But it does.   It does.   And now I'm working
        With *constellations!* What'll it *be,* Heaven? What new creature
    Would you *like* up there?   Listen, you universal son-of-a-bitch,
You're talking to a poet now, so don't give me a lot of shit.
        My old man was a God-damned astronomer
Of sorts
        —and didn't he say the whole sky's *invented?*

Well, I am now in*vent*ing.   You've *got* a Crab:
Especially tonight. I love to eat them: They scare me to death!
My head is smashed with *aquavit*,
And I've got a damn good Lobster in it   for   for
The Zodiac.   I'll send it right up.

And   listen now
I want *big* stars: some red   some white   some blue-white dwarves—
I want *everybody* to see my lobster! This'll be a *healing* lobster:
Not Cancer.   People will pray to him.   He'll have a good effect
On Time.

Now what I want to do is stretch him out

Jesus Christ, I'm drunk
I said stretch   stretch
Him out is what I said   stretch him out for millions
Of light years.   His eye   his eye

I'll make blue-white, so that the thing
Will cut and go deep and heal.   God, the *claws* that son-of-a-bitch

Is going to get from You! The clock-spire is telling me
To lie
for glory.   This is a poet talking to You
Like you talked to yourself, when you made all this up   while you conceived

The Zodiac. From every tower in Europe:
From my lifework and stupid travels and loneliness
And drunkenness, I'm changing the heavens
In my head. Get up there, baby, and dance on your claws:
On the claws God's going to give you.
I'm just before throwing up
All over myself.   I've failed again.   My lobster can't make it
To Heaven.   He's right here in town.   It must be the DT's.

You know, old lyre-picking buddy,
You in your whirling triangles, your terror of looking into a glass
Beside a light, your waking from ancient new-math,
To say, "Wretches, leave those beans alone," and "Do not eat the heart,"

72

You know   you know you've given me
Triangular eyes. You know that from the black death,
                                    of the forest of beast-
Symbols, the stars are beaten down by drunks

Into the page.
                        By GOD the poem is *in* there   out there
        Somewhere   the lines that will change
        Everything, like your squares and square roots
                Creating the heavenly music.
                                            It's somewhere,
Old great crazy thinker
                            ah
                                    farther down

In the abyss.   It takes triangular eyes

                To see Heaven.   I got 'em from you.
                                            All right,
I've got what I want, for now, at least.

                The paper staggers
From black to white to black, then to a kind of throbbing gold
                And blue, like the missal he read as a boy. It's like something
                                    He dreamed of finding
                In a cave, where the wellspring of creative blood
        Bubbles without death.
                            Where the hell *is* the light
Of the universe?   Gone out and around
        The world.   Oh my God

            You've got to look up
                            again: You've *got* to do it   you're committed
To it   look up   UP   you failed son of a bitch up MORE

                There it is
        Your favorite constellation
                        the hurdling-deep Hunter

Orion

With dim Alnilam sputtering in the middle.

                                        Well, but   quiet   why?
                        Why that one?   Why do you even remember
            The name?   The star's no good: not pretty,
        Not a good navigational aid.

                                    Ah, but secret.

                                        Ah, but central.

Let me explain it to you: that strange, overlooked, barely existing star

                        Is essential to the belt
Of the great, great Hunter.

                        Look.

                                    Just look.   The sword hangs down
The dog star travels on   on like European Christian soldiers going on

Before.

            The whole thing's hacked out
        Like cuneiform.   All right, so Orion's not in
            The Zodiac.   We'll *put* him in, along with some other things.
        He should never've been blackballed, even by Pythagoras.
            All right, friend, my friend myself, feel friendly
        Toward yourself.   It's possible, you know.   One more *aquavit*
            And you'll be entitled to breathe.

                                    He breathes

        Breathes deeply.

                        You know, like me, he says to the sideways
        Of the mobile,

                            the stars are gasping
                        For understanding.   They've *had* Ptolemy,
                        They've *had* Babylon

                                        but now they want Hubbell
        They want Fred Hoyle and the steady-state.

74

But what they really want   need
Is a poet   and
I'm going to have to be it.

And all the time I'm sitting here the astronomers are singing

Dies Irae, to the Day of Judgment's horn.
WHEN?

In all this immensity, all this telescope-country,
Why the microscopic searching
Of the useless human heart?

Why not die,

and breathe Heaven,
But not to have to *look* at it, not kill yourself trying to read it?

Except that there's relief   except
that there are birds.

There's one, a real *creature*, out there in a human city.
He's never seen a star
In his life, and if he has,

It didn't register.   There's no star-sound   star-silence
Around him.   He's in my main, starved winter tree,
He's the best thing I've got to my west.
When I look west I know
Everything's not over yet. I can always come back to earth.

But I want to come back with the secret
with the poem
That links up my balls and the strange, silent words
Of God   his scrambled zoo   and my own words
and includes the earth

Among the symbols.
Listen: you're talking to yourself
About Time: about clocks   spires   wheels: there are times

There is Time
Which the time-bell can't hold back
but gives
GIVES
Gives like vomit or diarrhea   but when it comes it is
The sound of new metal.

Well, all right.   Slowly the city drags and strays about in
Its wheedling darkness.

He looks up
From his paper-scrap   his overworked script   and,

Work-beast-white, he wanders to the window,
Getting himself brain-ready   ready for the pale-cell-game
He plays with the outside, when he turns his eyes down
Into trees, into human life,
into the human-hair gray,
Man's aging-hair-gray
Impenetrably thin   catching-up-with-and-passing the
never-all-there,
Going-toward-blackness   thornless
Thicket of twilight.

Words.

How?

II

A clock smash-bongs.   Stun.   Stun.
A spire's hiding out in the sound   tower-sound and now
      Floating over him and living on the nerve

      Of the instant, vibrating like a hangover:

      Time.

He waits.   God, I'm going to ask you one question:
      What do *wheels* and *machinery* have to do with Time?

With stars?   You know damn well I've never been able to master
      A watch-maker's laugh.
                        Overhead in the midst of Nothing,
Is the very clock for a drunk man.   For the Lord also?
Is it some kind of *compass?*   Is direction involved, maybe,
      Or is it nothing but the valve-grinding
Human noise of duration?   Do the wheels shift gears?
      If they do, then Time shifts gears.

      No; no:

Don't use that idea.
      It's simple enough, this town clock,
      The whole time-thing: after all
There's only this rosette of a great golden stylized asshole:

In human towns   in this one   in all of them—Ha! this is *our* symbol
      of eternity?
      Well, it's not good enough.

      Night.   Walking.   Time.
                        Nothing.
He goes on without anywhere to go. This is what you call Europe.

      Right?   The clock strokes pass
      Through him, aching like tooth-nerves, and he thinks

Our lives have been told, as long as we've had them,
                                        that the Father
                Must be torn apart in the son.
                                        Why?
                                                He swings up

                Through his eyes, and God

Whirls slowly in men's numbers   in the gilded Gothic
Of thorn-spiked Time.   What the hell: Can't eternity *stand* itself?
        Men caught that great wild creature minute
                        By shitty minute and smashed it down
                Into a rickety music box.
                                        Stun.   Stun.   Stun.
        The new hour's here.   He stares, aging, at new Time.

I know God-damned well it's not what they say it is:
                Clock-hands   heart-rhythm   moon-pulses   blood-flow of women—
No.
                Its just an uncreated vertigo
                Busted up by events.   Probably—now get this—
                The thing most like it is Cancer   both in and out

Of the Zodiac: everywhere existing in some form:
                In the stars   in works of art   in your belly,
                In the terrified breast of a woman,
                In your fate, or another's:
                                        the thing that eats.

                If Cancer dies overhead,
It dies everywhere.   Now try *that* one out, you and your ideas
                For poems.   Every poet wants
                To change those stars around.
                                        Look: those right *there:*
                Those above the clock.
                                        Religion, Europe, death, and the stars:
I'm holding them all in my balls, right now.
And the old *aquavit* is mixing them up—they're getting to know—

        78

They're *crazy* about each other!
Where God stood once in the stadium
Of European history, and battled mankind in the blue air
For domination, under the exploding Olympic-style flags
Of dawn, I'd put something *else* now:

something overhead.

God, at your best, you're my old—

You really *are* the water of life!   Look: here's what I'm going to do

For you. I'm going to swirl the constellation Cancer
Around like rice in a bucket, and out of that'll come a new beast

For the Zodiac!
I say right now, under the crashing clock, like a man
Bartending for God,
What'll it be?
Do you want me to decide?   The stars are mine as well as yours,
And don't forget it   and Christ
Would you tell me why my head keeps thinking
Up these half-assed, useless images?
Whiskey helps.
But it does.   It does.   Swirl on, sky! Now, I'm working
With constellations.   What'll it be, Heaven? What new earthly creature

Would you like up there?   Listen, you universal son of a bitch
You're talking to poet now, so don't give me a lot of shit.
You've got to remember that my old man
Was an astronomer, of sorts, and didn't he say the whole night sky's
invented?
Well, I am now *inventing*. You've *got* a crab.   Right?

How about a *Lobster* up there? With a snap of two right fingers
Cancer will whirl like an anthill   people will rise
Singing from their beds and take their wheaten children in their arms,

Who thought their parents were departing
For the hammer-clawed stars of death. They'll live

And live.   A *Lobster!* What an idea!   An idea God never had.   Listen, My God,
That thing'll be great!   He's coming into my head—
Is he inside or out?   No, I can *see* him!
The DT's aren't failing me: The light of Time shines on him
He's huge   he's a religious fanatic
He's gone wild because he can't go to Heaven
He's waving his feelers   his saw-hands
He's praying to the town clock   to minutes   millennia
He's praying the dial's stations of the Cross   he sees me
Imagination and dissipation both fire at me
Point-blank   O God, no   NO   I was playing   I didn't mean it
I'll never write it, I swear   CLAWS   claws   CLAWS

He's going to kill me.

III   Hallucination fading.   Underseas are tired of crawling
In a beast   waving claws for a drunk
Under man's dim, round Time.   Weird ring
Of city-time.   Well, now:
night hits a long stride.
There's the last tower-tone.   You might know it.
Bronze.
He feels it. The thing hurts. Time hurts. Jesus does it.
Man,
God-damn it,
you're one *too!*   Man   MAN   listen to me
Like God listened when he went mad
Over drunk lobsters.   This is Time, and more than that,
Time in Europe
Son of a bitch.
His life is shot   my life is shot.
It's also shit.   He knows it.   Where's it all gone off to?
The gods are in pieces
All over Europe.

But, by God, not *God*—

He sees himself standing up—

Dawn-rights.   How the hell did he ever get home?
         What home?   You call this white sty a *home?*
Yes, but *look* . . .
                    The vision's thorn-blue
                                   between a slope
And the hot sky.
                    And now his travels begin to swarm
         All over him.   He falls into clichés
         Right and left, from his windows! That remembered Greek blue
         Is *fantastic!*   That's all: no words
         But the ones anybody'd use: the one from humanity's garbage-can
Of language.
                    A poet has got to do better . . . *That* blue
                    Jesus, look at *that* in your memory!
         There   *there*   *that* blue   that *blue*
         Over some Demetrian island   something that's an island
                    More or less, with its present hour smoking

         Over it . . .   It's worth it all   worth it and lifted
         Into memory
                    he's lifted   he rises on the great, historical strength
         Of columns.   Look, you son of a bitch, I know what peace is,
         He says to his morning drink.   Peace, PEACE, you asshole . . .
         Look at me, mirror.   My *eyes* are full of it, of the pale blue fumes
         Of Mediterranean distance.   Isn't that *enough?*   The fresh stuff?
The old stuff . . .
                    —but, damn it, forgetting keeps moving in   closer.

         It's that thing you might call death.
                                   The walled, infinite
Peaceful-sea-beast-blue   moves in   in   it has a face

Bewildered, all-competent   everlasting   sure it will lie forever

Lie in the depths in distance-smoke: he's been there
        Among the columns:

                            among Europe. He can't tell Europe
From his own death, from his monstrous, peaceful   fierce
        Timelessness.   It follows like the images
        Of day-sleep.

                        Water-pressure   smoke   crabs
Lobsters.

            All RIGHT, reader, that's enough.   Let him go:

Let him go back to traveling   let him go on   in   onward   backward . . .

Ah, to hell with it: he can't quit.

                            Neither can you, reader.
He travels   he rises up
                        you with him, hovering on his shoulders,
                        A gas-fume reader   a gull a sleep and a smoke
        Of distance   a ruined column, riding him,
        His trapezius muscles in your deadly   your DT lobster's

        Your loving claws:
                        god-*damn*   it, he *can't* quit,
        But—*listen* to me—how can he *rise*
                    When he's *digging?* Digging through the smoke
        Of distance, throwing columns around to find   throwing
        To find   throwing distance   swaying   swaying into his head . . .
        He's drunk again.   Maybe that's all.   Maybe there's nothing maybe
        There's a mystery   mystery nearly got-to
        Now   NOW
                        No.
                    I can't get it.   Ah,
        But now he can think about his grave.   It's not so bad;
It will be better than this.   There's something there for him—
        At least it'll be in Europe, and he won't be sick
        For the impossible: with other-world nostalgia,
        With the countries of the earth.   Holland is good enough
        To die in.   That's the place to lay down

His screwed-up body-meat.   That's it.

                                    This is it.

It's that thing you might call home.

He moves.
                    While he's going

He sees the moon white-out. But it maintains itself
            Barely, in   some kind of thing

            Vibrating faintly with existence,   inside a crown
            Of desperate trees.   Image of Spring,

Old Buddy. But where in this neon,
Where in *hell* am I *going?* Well, it looks like I've come to some kind of

                    Lit-up ravine—

Well, what on God's earth *is* it?   I can barely make out
            A black church.   Now come on now: are you sure?

I can't cross it.   It moves across me
            Like an all-mighty stone.   But is it *universal?*
            The thing's been lifted from the beginning
                            Into this night-black—
                                            Into the Zodiac.

Without that hugely mortal beast   that multi-animal   animal
            There'd be no present time:
            Without the clock-dome, no city here,
            Without the axis and the poet's image   God's image
No turning stars   no Zodiac   without God's conceiving

            Of Heaven as beast-infested   Of Heaven in terms of beasts
            There'd be no calendar   dates   seasons

No Babylon   those abstractions that blitzed their numbers
   Into the Colosseum's crazy gates   and down

                                    down

   Into the woven beads that make the rosary
      Live   sing and swirl like stars

   Of creatures.

          Well, enough.   He loafs around
   The square.   He might be a cock-sucker
   Looking for trade.   He's got a platform   a springboard
   For himself . . .
          Nobody sees him;
                 nobody cares.

   He thinks he's sending night-letters
   To Mars, and yet he's looking straight
   Into the Milky Way   right now he's liking the hang of it—
   Now he's with Venus   he's getting a hard-on
         My God, look at that love-star   hammock-swaying
   Moving like an ass   moving the sky along.

V   Dark.

   Bed-dark.   The night can get at him here   and it comes,
 Tide after tide   and his nightmares rise and fall off him
      On the dry waves of the moon

      Thinking:
    The faster I sleep
   The faster the universe sleeps.
                And the deeper I breathe
  The higher the night can climb
             and the higher the singing will be.
  Bird, maybe?   *Night*ingale?   Ridiculous
             but over me

They're all one-eyed: the animals of light are in profile;
They're flat: God can't draw in depth
            When He uses constellations: the stars are beyond Him,
            Beyond his skill;   He can't handle them right.
                    A child could do better.
At the moment I'm passing truly
                        into sleep, a single star goes out

In each beast.
                Right.
                        The eye.
                                The eye, but can it be
That from the creative movement of the first light
On the face of the waters   from Time   from Genesis

The orbiting story   the insane mathematics   the ellipsis
Of history: the whole thing: time art life death stars
Love blood till the last fire explodes into dark
The last image   the candlestick the book and the lamb's fleece
Flame in delight at the longed-for end of it all
        Will flame in one human eye?   Right or left?   Well, old soul,
        What is it?
What does it mean, poet?   Is all this nothing but the clock-stunned light
Of my mind, or a kind of river-reflection of my basic sleep
Breaking down   sleeping down into reprisal-fear of God:
        The Zodiac standing over, pouring into
            The dreams that are killing me?

VI

Dreams, crossing the body, in out and around   crossing
                Whatever is left of me. What does that include?   Images:

Monsters.   Nothing else.   Monsters of stars.
The moon dies like a beast.   Not a stone beast or a statue:

A *beast*.   But it can't fall: it's in a gully of clouds,
A shameless place, like the rest of nature is.

At this idea, one part of his brain goes soft
As cloud, so the Lobster can come.

Soft brain, but the spirit turns to fire
Pure cosmic tetanus.   The sponge of his brain drinks it up:
        In the place where the thing is   seethes

The sweat of thought breaks out.
                                    It crowns him like a fungus:
        Idea of love.
                Love?
                    Yes, but who'll put a washrag on him?
                    It wouldn't matter; his whole skull's   broken out with it.
                    There's no sponge, no rag—

                    Poet's lockjaw: he can't speak: there's nothing

        Nothing for his mouth.

VII

            O flesh, that takes on any dirt
                    At all
                            I can't get you back in shape—
            It'd be better to go on being
            What I was   at one time or another: a plant
            In the dead-black flaming flowing
            Round flume of Time.

            Words fade before his eyes
            Like water-vapor, and the seed he thinks he's got available to give
                    Some woman, fades back
                    Deep into his balls, like a solar
                    Phenomenon, like cloud
                    Crossing the Goat—

He comes back, and some weird change comes on:
Our man may be getting double-sexed

Or something worse
                    or better—
                                but either way
His children are already murdered: they'll never *be* until the Goat
    Shines blindingly, and Time ends. Then, no,
            Either. Nothing will ever be.

            He says from his terrible star-sleep,
            Don't shack up with the intellect:
            Don't put your prick in a cold womb.
            Nothing but walking snakes would come of *that*—

            But if you conceive with meat

            Alone,
                    that child, too, is doomed.
            Look.   The moon has whited-out the script
                    Your hand drove into the paper.

            This poetry that's draining your bones
                    Of marrow has no more life
            Than the gray grass of public parks.

Leave it, and get out.   Go back to the life of a man.
    Leave the stars.   They're not saying what you think.
God is a rotten artist: he can't draw
With stars worth a shit   He can't say what He should
        To men   He can't say   speak   with   with
Stars what you want Him to
                            Ah, but the key *image*
Tonight   *tonight*
                is the gully   gullies:

Clouds make them, and other Realities
    Are revealed in Heaven, as clouds drift across,
Mysterious   sperm-colored:
                            Yes.

There, the world is original, and the Zodiac shines anew
    After every night-cloud.   New
With a nameless tiredness   a depth
    Of field I can't read   an oblivion with no bottom

    To it, ever, or never.

VIII

           Sun.   Hand-steadying brightness   Time
       To city-drift leg after leg, looking Peace
          In its empty eyes as things are beginning
             Already to go twelve hours
        Toward the other side of the clock, the old twilight
            When God's crazy beasts will come back.
           Death is twenty-eight years old
Today.   Somewhere in between sunrise
      And dusk he'll be bumming around.
                          Now he walks over water.
       He's on a bridge.   He feels truly rejected
                  but as he passes,
       Vacancy puts on his head
     The claw-hammer hair of terror.
              He moves along the slain canal
   Snoring in its bronze
Between docks.
      The fish, too,
  Are afraid of the sun
Under the half-stacked greens of the rotten bridge,
And light falls with the ultimate marigold horror:

  Innocence.
      The fish fin-flutter   able
Unable to hide their secrets any longer: what they know of Heaven
    As stars come down   come effortlessly down   down
Through water.   The trees are motionless, helping their leaves hold back

  Breath   life-death-breath—BACK: it's not time—

From the transparent rippling
    European story they've been told to tell
Themselves when everybody's dead
       they glitter the water.

   They shake with dawn-fear.

Again, his stepping stops him. No reason. Just does.
He's right here. Then he's drawn wavering into the fort
    Where the old house stands
On the vine-stalking hill. The town moat gets with the dawn,
    The morning loses time
Under the elm-heavy night, and in lost time drift the swans
     On-down, asleep.
He roams all the way round, one finger tracing
A house-size circle on the wall. The stone trembles scrambles—
    Comes clear: here was his room

    Here his mother twisted pain to death
    In her left breast—
    Above that wrung one window on the battle-tower
His father hauled, each night the Beasts had their one-eyes,
His telescope across the galleried desert-might of Heaven.
    Far, far beneath the body
Of his boy the cellar filled with rats. Their scrambling made his poor, rich youth
Shake all night, every night. His face and neck were like sponges
    Squeezed, slick with the green slime
    That gave the book-backs on his shelves
   Leprosy itself, and broke them out like relief-maps.
    The garden, he thinks, was here,
   Bald a few sparse elephant-head hairs.

  Where as a kid he'd ambled grumbling like a ghost
    In tulip shadow,
    The light humid cool

   Of the family maze.

IX

The garden where he hid the body—
His own—somewhere under the grape-roof—well,

Let him cry, and wipe his face on dead leaves
          Over the little bitch who filled, with *his* hand,
His diary with dreadful verses.

Why didn't he *do* it? That thing that scared him limp
          In daylight, that he did all night with himself?
          He should have screwed her or killed her
And he did—both—a hundred times. So would you.
          Sure, sure. He always put it off.   Nothing would happen.
Too late anyway.   Too shy.   She'd pass right by him in the street,
          Still, even if she saw him, joking with that asshole
          She married, who'd once been a school-god to him.

          Over.   All that's left of her is the dark of a home

She never visited.   There's no one in it; the man outside—myself—
          Is understanding he's in the business
                    Of doublecrossing his dreams.

The grave *of* youth?   HA!   *I told you:*   there's nobody *in* it!

          Why the hell did he come out here?

He lays his forehead on the salt stone-grains of the wall,
Then puts an ivy-leaf between. He turns his cheek.

          Outrage. Bare moon-stone. His ear's there
          And the rock prepares.   It stills   stills
          With his mother's voice. He grinds his hearing
          Into the masonry   it is   it is   it says
"Never come back here.
                              Don't wander around your own youth.
          Time is too painful here. Nothing stays with you
But what you remember."   The memory-animal crouched
Head-down   a huge lizard   in these vines, sleeping like winter,

Wrapped in dead leaves, lifts its eyes and pulls its lips back

Only at reunion.

He looks toward the window
Behind whose frozen glass he'd fucked
The first body he could get hold of.

Leaving skin, he tears himself off the wall.

Goodbye?
You're goddamned right, goodbye: this is *the* goodbye.

"You must leave here in every way," she'd said.
"When you feel the past draw you by the small intestine

You've got to go somewhere else.   Anywhere.
Somewhere no footstep has scrambled.   Go for the empty road."

"There's not any road," he says to the ivy
Massing with darkness behind him   that doesn't have tracks,
Most of them men's.   They've always been there."
He sees his mother laid-out in space,
Point to the moon. "That thing," she says,
"Puts man-tracks out like candles."
He gets all the way away

At last winding a little more
Than the garden path can wind.   He struggles in weeds,
Cursing, passing along
The piss-smell standing with the stable,
And reads on the first and last door,
Where his father's live
Starry letters had stood, a new

Designation   of somebody once human and here,
Now also moved away, dead, forgotten around too,

His long name harder than time.

X   Tenderness, ache on me,   and lay your neck
                On the slight shoulder-breathing of my arm . . .
                There's nobody to be tender with—
                This man has given up
                On anything stronger than he is.

                He's traveled everywhere
                But no place has ever done any good.
        What does his soul matter, saved like a Caesar-headed goldpiece,
                When the world's dying?

                He goes to the window,
        Hating everything, worn out, looking into the shook heart
                Of the city.

                Yet the stairwell hammers lightly
                Alive: a young step, nimble as foxfire,
                And the vital shimmer of a real face
                        Backs-off the white of the room.
        He closes his eyes, for the voice.
"My head is paralyzed with longing—"

He is quiet, but his arm is with her   around
        Her belly and tailbone.
His heart broods: he knows that nothing,
   Even love, can kill off his lonesomeness.

        Twilight passes, then night.

Their bodies are found by the dawn, their souls
        Fallen from them, left in the night
Of patterns   the night that's just finished
        Overwhelming the earth.

        Fading   fading   faded . . .

92

They lie like the expanding universe.

Too much light.   Too much love.

XI

A big room, a high one;
His first time in somebody else's.
Past the window, wind and rain
Paper-chasing each other to death,

And in the half-light one of Kandinsky's paintings
Squeezes art's blood out of the wallpaper.
His friend's voice rolls in his brain,
Rolls over and over
Joyfully, rapid-fire.   The lamp seeps on;
He thaws, forge-red like the stove,
Going blue with room-smoke—
And he shakes free of two years of wandering
Like melting-off European snows.

He *tells.*

He polar-bears through the room.
When he turns, a great grin breaks out.
The bottle pops its cork, and talk rushes over   rushes into
Cheese and gin   women   politics—
All changed   all the same . . .
Getting darker,
And by God, there's the *fish* market, gleaming its billion scales
Upward to him through the window.
More lights go on.
Where was he this time last year? He sees it:
Sees himself for a second at the Tetuan Friday Market,
And the *chalif,* through a double shine of trumpets,
Go into the tiny mosque.   It's all in pictures
In his friend's drunk-book.   He feels his last year, and his back
To the foreign wall. He turns page after page
Of the world   the post-cards he's sent,

93

Eagerly, desperately, looking for himself,
Tired, yellow with jaundice as an old portrait,

                       and something—

    That's it.   He's just heard an accordion:
      Two squeezed-lung, last-ditch
            First-ditch Dutch chords

    And he's back home.

XII

            A day like that.   But afterwards the fire
Comes straight down through the roof, white-lightning nightfall,
A face-up flash. Poetry. Triangular eyesight. It draws his
fingers together at the edge
Around a pencil.   He crouches bestially,
        The darkness stretched out on the waters
      Pulls back, humming Genesis. From wave-stars lifts
          A single island wild with sunlight,
      The white sheet of paper in the room.

He's far out and far in, his hands in a field of snow.
    He's making a black horizon with all the moves
    Of his defeated body. The virgin sheet becomes
More and more his, more and more another mistake,

But now, *now*
        Oh God you rocky landscape   give me,   Give
Me drop by drop
        desert water at least.
     I want now to write about deserts

    And in the dark the sand begins to cry
    For living water that not a sun or star
Can kill, and for the splay camel-prints that bring men,
    And the ocean with its enormous crooning, begs

    For haunted sailors   for refugees putting back
     Flesh on their ever-tumbling bones

To man that fleet,
                    for in its ships
            Only, the sea becomes the sea.

        Oh my own soul, put me in a solar boat.
            Come into one of these hands
            Bringing quietness and the rare belief
        That I can steer this strange craft to the morning
Land that sleeps   in the universe on all horizons
            And give this home-come man who listens in his room

        To the rush and flare of his father
    Drawn at the speed of light to Heaven
Through the wrong end of his telescope, expanding the universe,
        The instrument   the tuning-fork—
He'll flick it with his bandless wedding-finger—
        Which at a touch reveals the form
        Of the time-loaded European music
        That poetry has never really found,
    Undecipherable as God's bad, Heavenly sketches,
Involving fortress and flower, vine and wine and bone,

        And shall vibrate through the western world
So long as the hand can hold its island
        Of blazing paper, and bleed for its images:
        Make what it can of what is:

        So long as the spirit hurls on space
    The star-beasts of intellect and madness.

The Strength
of Fields

Root-light, or the Lawyer's Daughter

That any just to long for
The rest of my life, would come, diving like a lifetime
Explosion in the juices
Of palmettoes flowing
Red in the St. Mary's River as it sets in the east
Georgia from Florida off, makes whatever child
I was lie still, dividing
Swampy states   watching
The lawyer's daughter shocked
With silver   and I wished for all holds
On her like root-light. She came flying
Down from Eugene Talmadge
Bridge, just to long for as I burst with never
Rising never
Having seen her except where she worked
For J. C. Penney in Folkston. Her regular hours
Took fire, and God's burning bush of the morning
Sermon was put on her; I had never seen it where
It has to be. If you asked me how to find the Image
Of Woman to last
All your life, I'd say go lie
Down underwater for nothing
Under a bridge and hold Georgia
And Florida from getting at each other   hold
Like walls of wine. Be eight years old from Folkston ten
From Kingsland twelve miles in the clean palmetto color
Just as it blasts
Down with a body   red and silver buck
Naked with bubbles on Sunday   root
light explodes
Head-down, and there she is.

The Strength of Fields

. . . a separation from the world,
a penetration to some source of power
and a life-enhancing return . . .
Van Gennep: *Rites de Passage*

Moth-force a small town always has,

Given the night.

What field-forms can be,
Outlying the small civic light-decisions over
A man walking near home?
Men are not where he is
Exactly now, but they are around him   around him like the strength

Of fields.   The solar system floats on
Above him in town-moths.
Tell me, train-sound,
With all your long-lost grief,
what I can give.
Dear Lord of all the fields
what am I going to *do?*
Street-lights, blue-force and frail
As the homes of men, tell me how to do it   how
To withdraw   how to penetrate and find the source
Of the power you always had
light as a moth, and rising
With the level and moonlit expansion
Of the fields around, and the sleep of hoping men.

You?   I?   What difference is there?   We can all be saved

By a secret blooming. Now as I walk
The night   and you walk with me   we know simplicity
Is close to the source that sleeping men

Search for in their home-deep beds.

We know that the sun is away   we know that the sun can be conquered
By moths, in blue home-town air.
        The stars splinter, pointed and wild. The dead lie under
The pastures.   They look on and help.   Tell me, freight-train,
            When there is no one else
To hear.   Tell me in a voice the sea
    Would have, if it had not a better one: as it lifts,
        Hundreds of miles away, its fumbling, deep-structured roar
        Like the profound, unstoppable craving
        Of nations for their wish.
                            Hunger, time and the moon:

The moon lying on the brain
                        as on the excited sea   as on
    The strength of fields.   Lord, let me shake
With purpose.   Wild hope can always spring
From tended strength.   Everything is in that.
    That and nothing but kindness.   More kindness, dear Lord
Of the renewing green.   That is where it all has to start:
    With the simplest things.   More kindness will do nothing less
        Than save every sleeping one
        And night-walking one

Of us.
        My life belongs to the world. I will do what I can.

Two Poems of the Military

I. Haunting the Maneuvers

Prepared for death and unprepared
For war, there was Louisiana   there was Eisenhower a Lieutenant
Colonel and there was I
As an Invasion Force.   The Defenders were attacking
And I was in the pinestraw
Advancing   inching through the aircraft of the Home
Force.   Sacks of flour were bursting
All over the trees. Now if one of them damned things hits you in the head
It's gonna kill you just as sure as if
It was a real bomb
So watch it.   Yes Sir.   I was watching
It.   One sack came tumbling after
Me no matter
What.   Not in the head,   though,
I thought thank God at least
Not dead.
But I was dead.   The sergeant said go sit
Over there: you are the first man killed.   It's KP for you
For the whole rest of the war.   This war,
Anyway.   Yes Sir.   The Defenders had struck
The first blow: I was plastered.   I thought why this
Is easy: there's not a drop
Of blood there's only death
White on me; I can live
Through.
I lived through in the Hell
Of latrine duty, but mostly on KP, on metal
Trays that dovetailed to each other, stacked by the ton in the field
Kitchens. I moved them all at one time
Or other, and the Defenders
Ate   ate and went back to killing
My buddies with blanks and bread. But when I slept on that well
Defended ground   the pinestraw stirred   each needle pointed up

Into the dark like a compass, and white   whiter
Than my skin, edible, human-eyed through the pines,
Issued a great mass
Laugh   a great lecture-laugh by the chaplain's one
Dirty joke, I rose
Over the unprepared boys   over the war
Games the war
Within a war   over the trucks with mystical signs
On them that said TANK   over World War One
Enfield rifles filled with dud rounds   self-rising
Through the branches   driven up like a small cloud
Of the enemy's food   at the same time bread

And bomb, swanned out like a diver, I came
From my death over both sleeping armies,
Over Eisenhower dreaming of invasion.   Where are you,
My enemy?   My body won't work any more
For you: I stare down like stars
Of yeast: you will have to catch me
And eat me.   Where are you, invading
Friends?   Who else is dead?   O those who are in this
With me, I can see nothing
But what is coming   can say
Nothing but what the first-killed
Working hard all day for his vision
Of war says best: the age-old Why
In God's name Why
In Louisiana, Boys   O Why
In Hell are we doing this?

II.   Drums Where I Live

So that sleeping and waking
Drum, drum, every day the first part of the sun,
Its upper rim
And rhythm, I live here. I and my family pass, in the new house,
Into the great light mumbling one
Two three four, marching in place like boys

Laid out, all voices of the living and the dead
To come and hovering
Between brought in
to cadence.   It is not
A heart, but many men.   Someone said it is
Comfort, comforting to hear them.   Not every
Sun-up, neighbor: now and then I wish I had a chance
To take my chances
With silence. More and more
They seem to be waiting
For the day   more and more as my son sighs all over the house
Intercom.   I know, I know: he is counting
His years.   When we rise, the drums
Have stopped. But I know from the jungle of childhood
Movies what that means. There is nothing in the grenades'
Coming-closer bursts to worry
Anyone; they are Expanding
The Range.   It is only in the morning
Paper that a trainee hangs himself
On the obstacle course.   And it is nothing but nerves
That make something human, a cry,
Float like a needle on the sunlight
From the stockade.   But every night I sleep assured
That the drums are going
To reach me at dawn like light
Where I live, and my heart, my blood and my family will assemble
Four barely-livable counts.   Dismissed,
Personnel.   The sun is clear
Of Basic Training.   This time, this
Is my war and where in God's
Name did it start?   In peace, two, three, four:
In peace peace peace peace

One two

In sleep.

The Voyage of the Needle

The child comes sometimes with his mother's needle
And draws a bath with his hand.   These are your fifty years
                    Of fingers, cast down among
                    The hard-driven echoes of tile
In the thresholding sound of run water.   Here the sun divides light
            From the Venetian sector of the dark
Where you sink through both,
                              and warmly, more slowly than being
Smoothed and stretched, your bodying barge-ripples die.
                    A gauze of thin paper upholds
            The needle, then soaks like an eyelid
                    And falls, uncontrolling, away.
                                        The hung metal voyages alone,
            Like the trembling north-nerve of a compass,
On surface tension, that magic, like a mother's spell
Cast in sharp seed in your childhood, in scientific trickery rooted
And flowering in elation. It is her brimming otherworld
That rides on the needle's frail lake, on death's precarious membrane,
            Navigating through all slanted latitudes,
                    Containing a human body
            She gave, and saved to bear, by a spell
        From physics, this fragile cargo.   "Mother," you say,
                "I am lying in a transference
                    Of joy and glory: come to me
        From underground, from under the perilous balance
                    Of a thicket of thorns.   I lie
As unmoving. Bring the needle to breathless harbor
                Somewhere on my body, that I may rise
                    And tell. My sex is too deep,
My eyes too high for your touch. O let it reach me at the lips'
            Water-level, the thorns burst
        Into rain on your wooded grave, the needle plunge
Through the skin of charmed water and die, that I may speak at last
                    With up-bearing magic
                Of this household, weightless as love."

The Rain Guitar

—England, 1962—

The water-grass under had never waved
But one way.   It showed me that flow is forever
Sealed from rain in a weir.   For some reason having
To do with Winchester, I was sitting on my guitar case
Watching nothing but eelgrass trying to go downstream with all the right motions
But one. I had on a sweater, and my threads were opening
Like mouths with rain. It mattered to me not at all
That a bridge was stumping
With a man, or that he came near and cast a fish
thread into the weir.   I had no line and no feeling.
I had nothing to do with fish
But my eyes on the grass they hid in, waving with the one move of trying
To be somewhere else. With what I had, what could I do?
I got out my guitar, that somebody told me was supposed to improve
With moisture—or was it when it dried out?—and hit the lowest
And loudest chord.   The drops that were falling just then
Hammered like Georgia railroad track
With E.   The man went into a kind of fishing
Turn.   Play it, he said through his pipe.   There
I went, fast as I could with cold fingers.   The strings shook
With drops.   A buck dance settled on the weir.   Where was the city
Cathedral in all this?   Out of sight, but somewhere around.
Play a little more
Of that, he said, and cast.   Music-wood shone,
Getting worse or better faster than it liked:
Improvement or disintegration
Supposed to take years, fell on it
By the gallon.   It darkened and rang
Like chimes. My sweater collapsed, and the rain reached
My underwear. I picked, the guitar showered, and he cast to the mountain
Music.   His wood leg tapped
On the cobbles.   Memories of many men
Hung, rain-faced, improving, sealed-off

In the weir.   I found myself playing Australian
Versions of British marching songs.   Mouths opened all over me; I sang,
His legs beat and marched
Like companions.   I was Air Force,
I said.   So was I; I picked
This up in Burma, he said, tapping his gone leg
With his fly rod, as Burma and the South
west Pacific and North Georgia reeled,
Rapped, cast, chimed, darkened and drew down
Cathedral water, and improved.

Remnant Water

Here in the thrust-green

Grass-wind and thin surface now nearly
Again and again for the instant

Each other   hair-lined backwater barely there and it
    Utterly:
              this that was deep flashing—
    Tiny grid-like waves   wire-touched water—
    No more, and comes what is left

    Of the gone depths duly arriving
Into the weeds belly-up:
             one carp now knowing grass
    And also thorn-shucks and seeds
   Can outstay him:
           next to the slain lake the inlet
   Trembles   seine-pressure in something of the last
     Rippling   grass in the slow-burning

    Slow-browning dance learned from green;
   A hundred acres of canceled water come down
    To death-mud shaking
Its one pool   stomach-pool   holding the dead one diving up
Busting his gut in weeds   in scum-gruel glowing with belly-white
Unhooked   around him all grass in a bristling sail taking off back-
   blowing.   Here in the dry hood I am watching
  Alone, in my tribal sweat   my people gone my fish rolling
      Beneath me   and I die
      Waiting   will wait out
    The blank judgment given only
In ruination's suck-holing acre   wait and make the sound surrounding NO

Laugh primally: be
Like an open-gut flash   an open under-
water eye with the thumb
pressure to brain the winter-wool head of me,
Spinning my guts with my fish in the old place,
Suffering its consequences, dying,
Living up to it.

Two Poems of Flight-Sleep

I. Camden Town

—Army Air Corps,
Flight Training, 1943—

With this you trim it.   Do it right and the thing'll fly
Itself.   Now get up there and get those lazy-
eights down.   A check-ride's coming at you
Next week.
                I took off in the Stearman like stealing two hundred and twenty horses
Of escape from the Air Corps.
                                    The cold turned purple with the open
Cockpit, and the water behind me being
The East, dimmed out.   I put the nose on the white sun
And trimmed the ship.   The altimeter made me
At six thousand feet.   We were stable: myself, the plane,
The earth everywhere
Small in its things with cold
But vast beneath.   The needles on the panel
All locked together, and a banner like World War One
Tore at my head, streaming from my helmet in the wind.
I drew it down   down under the instruments
Down where the rudder pedals made small corrections
Better than my feet   down where I could ride on faith
And trim, the aircraft slightly cocked
But holding the West by a needle.   I was in
Death's baby machine, that led to the fighters and bombers,
But training, here in the lone purple,
For something else.   I pulled down my helmet-flaps and droned
With flight-sleep.   Near death
My watch stopped.   I knew it, for I felt the Cadet
Barracks of Camden die like time, and "There's a war on"
Die, and no one could groan from the dark of the bottom
Bunk to his haggard instructor, I tried
I tried to do what you said   I tried   tried

No;   never.   No one ever lived to prove he thought he saw
An aircraft with no pilot showing: I would have to become
A legend, curled up out of sight with all the Western World
Coming at me under the floor-mat, minute after minute, cold azures,
                    Small trains and warbound highways,
All entering flight-sleep.   Nothing mattered but to rest in the winter
                    Sun beginning to go
Down early.   My hands in my armpits, I lay with my sheep-lined head
                    Next to the small air-moves
Of the rudder pedals, dreaming of letting go   letting go
The cold   the war   the Cadet Program and my peanut-faced
Instructor and his maps.   No maps   no world   no love
But this.   Nothing can fail when you go below
The instruments.   Wait till the moon.   Then.   Then.
But no.   When the waters of Camden Town died, then so
Did I, for good.   I got up bitterly, bitter to be
                    Controlling, re-entering the fast colds
Of my scarf, and put my hands and feet where the plane was made
For them.   My goggles blazed with darkness as I turned,
And the compass was wrenched from its dream
                    Of all the West.   From luxurious
                    Death in uncaring I swung
                    East, and the deaths and nightmares
                    And training of many.

II.   Reunioning Dialogue

—New York, 1972,
St. Moritz bar—

Didn't we double!

                    Sure, when we used to lie out under the wing
            Double-teaming the Nips near our own hole
            In the ground   opening an eye

For the Southern Cross, and we'd see something cut the stars

Out into some kind of shape, the shape of a new Widow

111

Black Widow
> and all over the perimeter the ninety millimeters would open

> *Up on Heaven   the sirens would go off*
And we'd know better than not to dive
> > for the palm logs,
> The foxhole filled with fear-slime, and lie there,
Brains beating like wings
> > *our new wings from Northrop,*
> *The enemy looking for the aircraft*
We slept under.
> > Well, we knew what we wanted,
Didn't we?
> > *To get out from under our own wings,*
To let them lift us
> > *together*
> > > lift us out of the sleep
With a hole in it, and slot back fresh windows and climb in the squared-off   cool

Of the Cross.
> Angels, Observer!
> > *Nine thousand angels,*
Pilot! The altitude of the Heavenly Host

> *In the Philippines is that completely air-conditioned*
Nine thousand feet!
> I couldn't wait to fool with the automatic pilot,

And I went absolutely crazy over Howard Hughes' last word
In radar!
> *Remember?*
> > *We were pulling convoy cover.*
By my figures we were seven hundred miles south of base, my eyes brilliant sweeps
Of electronic yellow, watching the spinner painting-in the fleet,
The arranged, lingering images of the huge fortunes
Of war   the great distances and secret relationships
Between tankers and troopships   and on my screen, God's small, brilliant chess-set
Of world war, as we sat

Circling
                 relaxing in all the original freshness
       Of the Cross, comfortable and light
And deadly: night-cool of nine thousand angels
Over the fleet.
                You called back with clear, new
       Electricity: Hey, Buddy, how're you liking this?
What a war!   I said.   The scope just pulses away
Like a little old yellow heart.   The convoy comes in, the convoy goes out
     And comes right back in for you and me
         And Uncle Sam.
                     It was easy,
    Right?   Milk run?   Why, by God, we *flew* on milk!
      I cut-in the automatic pilot and leaned back
In the cool of those southern stars, and could have spent the rest of my life
        Watching the gyros jiggle the wheel
     With little moves like an invisible man   like a ghost
   Was flying us.   The next thing I knew the intercom busted in
   With YOU   I looked down and out
                   I looked the radar down
To the depths of its empty yellow heart.   I didn't have a ship
      To my name.
                And I said where in Hell
   Are we?   Jesus God, I was afraid of my watch   afraid to look
    Afraid the son of a bitch had stopped.   But no,
       Four hours had gone to Hell
  Somewhere in the South Pacific.   Our engines were sucking wind,
   Running on fumes, and I started calling everything that had a code
Name south of our island.   Nothing.   But I thought of the five boys
     From our squadron   all volleyball players
      With no heads, and all but one
Island south of us was Japanese.   I thought I could hear the sword swish,
       But it was a wisp arriving
    In my earphones   an American spirit crackling
  That we were over Cebu.   They had one strip and no lights,
     Lumps and holes in the runway and the moon

Almost gone.   I said to the Seabees get me a couple of things
            That burn;   I'll try to come down between 'em.

            —Can you hold out for fifteen minutes?—

Just about.

                They doubled.   Two pairs of lights came running.
Together   then split   stopped and gave us five thousand devilish feet
            Of blackness laid out maybe on the ground. I said hold on,
                Buddy;   this may just be it.   We drifted in   full
Flaps   nose-high   easing   easing   cleared the first lighted jeep

                    Hit and

                Bounced   came down again hit a hole
            And double-bounced   the great new night-
            gathering binoculars came unshipped and banged me in the head
                As I fought for hot, heavy ground,
                Trying to go straight for the rest of my life
                For the other jeep,
                Doing anything and everything to slaughter
                The speed, and finally down
            Got down to the speed of a jeep   down
            Down and turned off into the bushes that'd been pouring
                By   pouring with sweat and killed
            The engine.   Man, was I shaking!   I couldn't even undo the hatch.
                You pounded at me
        From underneath.   I'm all right, I said, drawing in the stuffed heat of life,
            Of my life. I climbed down, rattling the new black
California bolts of the wings.

                        Buddy, would you sit there and tell me,
            How we got over Cebu?   Why, it was the wrong goddamned *island!*
                Why didn't you give me a course
        Correction?   Our million dollar Black Widow bird like to've carried us off
                And killed us!   How come you didn't say a thing
                For four hours?

I'm sorry, Pilot, but that Southern Cross
Had the most delicious lungs
For me.   We'd jumped out of our hole
On wings   the heat was off   and weight, and I could breathe
At last.   I was asleep.

Well, for the Lord's sake,
Observer   Navigator   Miracle
Map-reader   second half of the best
Two-man crew in night-fighters, as we sit here
In Central Park, where on earth in that war
Have we *been?*

I don't know.   I told you I was asleep.

Well, Old Buddy, the ghosts had us
For sure, then.   Ghosts and angels.   Nobody else.
I guess   in Central Park   I can tell you, too, after all
These years.   So was I.

For the Death of Lombardi

I never played for you.   You'd have thrown
Me off the team on my best day—
No guts, maybe   not enough speed,
Yet running in my mind
As Paul Hornung, I made it here
With the others, sprinting down railroad tracks,
Hurdling bushes and backyard Cyclone
Fences, through city after city, to stand, at last, around you
Exhausted,   exalted, pale
As though you'd said "Nice going":   pale
As a hospital wall.   You are holding us
Millions together: those who played for you, and those who entered the bodies
Of Bart Starr, Donny Anderson, Ray Nitchke, Jerry Kramer
Through the snowing tube on Sunday afternoon,
Warm, playing painlessly
In the snows of Green Bay Stadium, some of us drunk
On much-advertised beer   some old   some in other
Hospitals—most, middle-aged
And at home.   Here you summon us, lying under
The surgical snows.   Coach, look up: we are here:
We are held in this room
Like cancer.
                    The Crab has you, and to him
And to us you whisper
Drive, *Drive*.   Jerry Kramer's face floats near—real, pale—
We others dream ourselves
Around you, and far away in the mountains, driving hard
Through the drifts, Marshall of the Vikings, plunging   burning
Twenty-dollar bills to stay alive, says, still
Alive, "I wouldn't be here
If it weren't for the lessons of football." Vince, they've told us:
When the surgeons got themselves
Together and cut loose
Two feet of your large intestine, the Crab whirled up   whirled out
Of the lost gut and caught you again

116

Higher up.   Everyone's helpless
But cancer.   Around your bed the knocked-out teeth like hail-pebbles
Rattle down   miles of adhesive tape from hands and ankles
Writhe in the room like vines   gallons of sweat blaze in buckets
In the corners   the blue and yellow of bruises
Make one vast sunset around you.   No one understands you.
Coach, don't you know that some of us were ruined
For life?   Everybody can't win.   What of almost all
Of us, Vince?   We lost.   And our greatest loss was that we could not survive
Football. Paul Hornung has withdrawn
From me, and I am middle-aged and gray, like these others.
What holds us here?   It is that you are dying by the code you made us
What we are by.   Yes, Coach, it is true: love-hate is stronger
Than either love or hate.   Into the weekly, inescapable dance
Of speed, deception, and pain
You led us, and brought us here weeping.
But as men.   Or, you who created us as George
Patton created armies, did you discover the worst
In us: aggression   meanness   deception   delight in giving
Pain to others, for money?   Did you make of us, indeed,
Figments   over-specialized, brutal ghosts
Who could have been real
Men in a better sense?   Have you driven us mad
Over nothing?   Does your death set us free?

Too late.   We stand here among
Discarded TV commercials:
Among beer-cans and razor-blades and hair-tonic bottles,
Stinking with male deodorants: we stand here
Among teeth and filthy miles
Of unwound tapes, novocaine needles, contracts, champagne
Mixed with shower-water, unraveling elastic, bloody faceguards,
And the Crab, in his new, high postion
Works soundlessly.   In dying
You give us no choice, Coach,
Either.   We've got to believe there's such a thing
As winning.   The Sunday spirit-screen
Comes on   the bruise-colors brighten   deepen

117

On the wall   the last tooth spits itself free
Of a line-backer's aging head   knee-cartilage cracks,
A boy wraps his face in a red jersey and crams it into
A rusty locker to sob, and we're with you
We're with you all the way
You're going forever, Vince.

False Youth: Autumn: Clothes of the Age

—for Susan Tuckerman Dickey—

Three red foxes on my head, come down
There last Christmas from Brooks Brothers
As a joke, I wander down Harden Street
In Columbia, South Carolina, fur-haired and bald,
Looking for impulse in camera stores and redneck greeting cards.
A pole is spinning
Colors I have little use for, but I go in
Anyway, and take off my fox hat and jacket
They have not seen from behind yet.   The barber does what he can
With what I have left, and I hear the end man say, as my own
Hair-cutter turns my face
To the floor, Jesus, if there's anything I hate
It's a middle-aged hippie.   Well, so do I, I swallow
Back: so do I   so do I
And to hell.   I get up, and somebody else says
When're you gonna put on that hat,
Buddy?   Right now.   Another says softly,
Goodbye, Fox.   I arm my denim jacket
On and walk to the door, stopping for the murmur of chairs,
And there it is
hand-stitched by the needles of the mother
Of my grandson   eagle riding on his claws with a banner
Outstretched as the wings of my shoulders,
Coming after me with his flag
Disintegrating, his one eye raveling
Out, filthy strings flying
From the white feathers, one wing nearly gone:
Blind eagle but flying
Where I walk, where I stop with my fox
Head at the glass to let the row of chairs spell it out
And get a lifetime look at my bird's
One word, raggedly blazing with extinction and soaring loose

In red threads burning up white until I am shot in the back
Through my wings   or ripped apart
For rags:

Poetry.

For the Running of the New York City Marathon

If you would run

If you would quicken the city with your pelting,
        Then line up, be counted, and change
Your body into time, and with me through the boxed maze flee
        On soft hooves, saying   all saying in flock-breath
        Take me there.
                                I am against you
                And with you: I am second
Wind and native muscle in the streets   my image lost and discovered
        Among yours: lost and found in the endless panes
                Of a many-gestured bald-headed woman, caught between
        One set of clothes and tomorrow's: naked, pleading in her wax
                For the right, silent words to praise
                The herd-hammering pulse of our sneakers,
        And the time gone by when we paced
River-sided, close-packed in our jostled beginning,
        O my multitudes.
                                We are streaming from the many to the one
                At a time, our ghosts chopped-up by the windows
Of merchants;   the mirroring store-fronts let us, this one day,
                Wear on our heads feet and backs
        What we would wish.   This day I have taken in my stride
                Swank jogging-suits rayed with bright emblems
        Too good for me: have worn in blood-sweating weather
        Blizzard-blind parkas and mukluks, a lightning-struck hairpiece
        Or two, and the plumes of displayed Zulu chieftains.

Through the colors of day I move as one must move
                His shadow somewhere on
Farther into the dark.   Any hour now   any minute
                Attend the last rites
                Of pure plod-balance!   Smoke of the sacrificial
Olympic lamb in the Deli!   O swooping and hairline-hanging
        Civic-minded placement of bridges!   Hallelujas of bars!

Teach those who have trained in the sunrise
On junk-food and pop, how to rest   how to rise
From the timed city's never-die dead.   Through the spattering echo
Of Vulcanized hundreds, being given the finish-line hot-foot,
I am lolloping through to the end,
By man-dressing mannequins clad   by flashes of sun on squared rivers
As we breast our own breathless arrival: as we home in,
Ahead of me   me   and behind me
All winning over the squirrel-wheel's outlasted stillness, on the unearthly pull and fall
Of our half-baked soles, all agony-
smiles and all winning—

All winning, one after one.

Exchanges

(Phi Beta Kappa Poem, Harvard, 1970)

> —being in the form of a dead-living dialogue with
> Joseph Trumbull Stickney (1874–1904)—
> (Stickney's words are in italics)

Under the cliff, green powered in from the open,
      Changed   and she
    And I crouched at the edge
Five hundred feet above the ocean's suicide in a bubble
And horizon of oil.   Smog and sweet love!   We had the music for the whale-
death of the world.   About us the environment crumbled
      In yellow light.   There was no forth-
coming of wave-silver, but silver would flash now
And then through, turning side-on in many mullet
      To the sun to die, as I tuned
    The wild guitar.   This won't get any worse
      Until tomorrow, I said
    Of Los Angeles, gazing out through "moderate eye
damage"   twisting the pegs   and under the strings

—The gray crane spanned his level, gracious flight

    Knowing better than to come
    To rest on anything, or touch
    Zuma Point here and now.

—O sea

Of California, thou Pacific,
For which the multitude of mortals bound
Go trembling headlong and with terrific
Outcry are drowned:
      Day-moon meant more
Far from us   dazing the oil-slick with the untouched remainder

Of the universe   spreading   contracting
Catching fish at the living end
In their last eye   the guitar rang moon and murder
And Appalachian love, and sent them shimmering from the cliff

                    —*The burning season shone*
On the vast feather-shapes of the open
            Sea tranquilized by off-
    shore drilling
                            where gulls flapped in black
            Gold   black
            Magic of corporations—

    —*So here did mix the land's breath and the sea's:*
            Among the beautiful murders
                Showering down ballad
After ballad on the rainbows of forever lost
Petroleum that blew its caps and turned on
All living things, we sang and prayed for purity, scattered everywhere
                    Among the stones
    Of other worlds   and asked the moon to stay off us
        As far as it always had, and especially far
        From L.A.   I playing from childhood also
Like the Georgia mountains   the wind out of Malibu whipped her
Long hair into "Wildwood Flower"   her blue eye   —*whose eye*
        Was somewhat strangely more than blue
            Closed
                        —*and if we lived*
    We were the cresting of a tide wherein
    An endless motion rose exemplified.
                                    In

        —*The gentle ecstasy of earth*
    And ruination, we lay on the threatened grass
Of cliffs, she tangled in my strings, her dark hair tuned
        To me, the mountains humming back
        Into resolution, in the great low-crying key
        Of A.

124

—I saw the moon and heard her sing.
I saw her sing and heard the moon.

O vibrating mountains and bronze
Strings, O oil-slicks in the moderately damaged eye
And the sides of fish flashing out
One more time   birds black with corporations, turn me over to those

—Maddened with hunger for another world:
                                 She lies in Glendale,
      In Forest Lawn.
                               O astronauts,
            Poets, all those
Of the line of wizards and saviors, spend your lives
And billions of dollars to show me
The small true world
Of death, the place we sang to,
From Zuma.   I read and imagine everything
I can of the gray airless ground
Of the moon   sphere cracked and bombarded
By negation   pure death, where death has not
Yet come
         —where yet no God appears:
                               Who knows?
There might be some unknown
Consolation in knowing California
Is not the deadest world of all
Until tomorrow: might be some satisfaction
Gone spatial   some hope
Like absolute zero, when the earth can become

      —The last of earthly things
Carelessly blooming in immensity
                          and live men ride
Fleeing outward

      —a white flame tapering at the core of space   their hatches
      —Firm-barred against the fearful universe   until

In the easy-leaping country
Of death, beings   *—still armored in their visionary gold*
Do human deeds.
What deeds?

Will Los Angeles rise from the Sea
Of Tranquillity, on a great bubble
Of capped breath and oil?   Not yet;
The first men will see that desolation
Unimproved, before the freeways
Link it to Earth. Ah, to leap or lie
On some universal ruin
Not ruined by us!   To be able to say—*Am I dead*
That I'm so far?
But where I stand,
Here, under the moon, the moon
—Breaks desperate magic on the world I know,

On Glendale.   *—All through the shadows crying grows, until*
The wailing is like grass upon the ground.
It is I

Howling like a dog for the moon, for Zuma Point no matter what
The eye-damage   howling to bring her back note
By note like a childhood mountain
In the key of A   or, lacking that, howling
For anything   for the ultimate death   pure death
For the blaze of the outer dark   for escape
From L.A. smoldering and eye-
burning along the freeways   from rubber-smoke
And exhaust streaming *into the endless shadow*
Of my memory.   *—Let me grind alone*
And turn my knuckles in the granite
Of the moon
where underfoot the stones
—wild with mysterious truth
lie in their universal

Positions, in a place of no breath
And one machine

and for these reasons and many
Another I was quartered and drawn
To Cape Canaveral, with my tangled dream of Los Angeles
And death and the moon, my dead girl still tuned to me
In my tangled guitar.   The environment crumbled
In red light, and raised up by dawn
Almighty buildings.

I felt a time-like tremor in my limbs.
I wished to be bound that morning
For the true dead land, the land made to sustain
No life at all, giving out the unruined light
That shines on the fish-slicks of Zuma.

—Are we the people of the end?

Before us all

The sun burst
From a machine   timed   slowly   tilting   leaning
Upward   drawn moonward inch by inch   faster
Faster   a great composite roar battered
Like a board at the very bone
Marrow, and in the hardshell case
I sat on, the strings vibrated not with
Mountains   but made the shapeless and very
Music of the universal
Abyss

—and all the air
Was marvelous and sorrowful

as we beheld,
Exploding with solitude   blasting into the eyes and body,
Rising   rising in dreadful machine-
pain as we prayed   as the newsmen fell to their knees   as the quality of life
And death changed forever
For better or worse
—Apollo springing naked to the light.

127

Nothing for me
Was solved.   I wandered the beach
Mumbling to a dead poet
In the key of A, looking for the rainbow
Of oil, and the doomed
Among the fish.
—Let us speak softly of living.

Head-Deep in Strange Sounds:
Free-Flight Improvisations
from the unEnglish

Purgation

—Po Chu-yi—

Beyond the eye, grasses go over the long fields.
Every season it happens, as though I—no; I and you,
Dear friend—decreed it.   It is what we would like to have,

And it is there.
                  It is the season for wildfire,
And it will come, but will never quite get every one
Of the grasses.   There is some green left, this year as last,

For us.   Once more they are tall
In the April wind.   They make the old road *be*

The road, where you and I go toward the old, beetle-eaten
City gate.   Oh, fire, come *on!*   I trust you.

My ancient human friend, you are dead, as we both know.
But I remember, and I feel the grass and the fire
Get together in April   with you and me, and that
Is what I want   both age-gazing living and dead

     both sighing like grass and fire.

The Ax-God: Sea Pursuit

—after Alfred Jarry—

On the horizon, through the steam of exhausted blast-furnaces   fog   Yes
Pure Chance blows, as though it were really itself   blows
Not very well, and moans and shakes bells.

These are the sounds that invented salt.   But, listen,
Waves, we are among the arced demons you are hiding

In the visiting green gullies of your mountains.
Where the shoreline clamps a lost quivering over all
Of us, a huge and shadow-cast shape looms over muck.
We crawl round his feet, loose as lizards,

While, like a filthy Caesar on his chariot,
Or on a marble, leg-crossing plinth,
Carving a whale-boat from a tree-trunk, he . . .

Well, in that branching boat, he'll run
Us down, league for league   down   down to
The last of the sea's center-speeding
Center-spreading and ropeless knots.   Green   blue   white
Time space distance: starting from the shore

His arms of unhealable, veined copper   over us
Raise to Heaven a breathing blue ax.

Nameless

(near Eugenio Montale)

Sure.   All the time I come up on the evil
                                    of just living:

It's been the strangled creek that still tries
To bubble like water   it's been the death-rattling leaf
Dried out for no reason
                              and the tripped-sprawling horse.

As for anything good: you find it for me
And I'll look at it.   All I can come up with
Is an enclosure: the religion-faking sun-blasted rack
Of divine Indifference.   As I say, Sure:

It's the statue in its somnolescence
Of primitive, hectored stone.   It's noon

And cloud   and the falcon in circles,
Who planes, as high as he can get,

                              For nothing.

Math

—Lautréamont—

Numbers who can't ever hear me
                    I'll say it anyway
All the way from my age-old school.   You're still in my heart,
     And I can feel you go through there
Like a clean sea-wave.   I breathed-in, instinctively,
From the one-two, one-two counts
     Of the soft-rocking cradle

     As drinking from a universal spring
                         older than the sun:

Numbers.   There is this wave of matched, watched numbers
In my school-soul.   Sometimes it is like smoke: I can't get through it.
Sometimes I believe that you've put   put in place of my heart
Inhuman logic.   Coldness
                         beyond bearing.   And yet . . . because of you
My intelligence has grown far beyond me
                         from the frozen, radiant center
Of that ravishing clarity you give: give to those
     Who most truly love you   and can find you: *Listen*, ever-deaf numbers.
                              Hail!   *I* hail you
               Arithmetic!   Algebra!   Geometry!

               Triangle gone luminous!

Judas

—Georg Heym, resurrected from
under the ice—

Mark.   Hair, one strand of it, can curl
Over your forehead like a branding-iron.
And meaningless winds   and many voices can be whispering
Like creek-flow, staying and going by.

But he runs close to His side like a mongrel,
And in the sick mud he picks up everything said
To him, and weighs it in his quivering hands.
                              It is dead.

Ah, most gently in the swaying dusk,
The Lord walked down
Over the white fields.   Ear by ear, green by green,
Yellow by yellow, the corn-ears, the stalks, the sheer *growing*
Glorified.   His feet were as small as houseflies, as they were perpetually being

Sent-down step by step
                    From the golden hysteria of Heaven.

135

Small Song

—from the Hungarian of Attila Jozsef,
head crushed between two boxcars—

I'm laughing, but being very quiet about it.
I've got my pipe and my knife:
I am quiet, and laughing like hell.

All hail, Wind!   Let my song fall in jigsaw fragments!
Nobody is my friend except the one who can say
"I take pleasure in his misery."

I am of shadow and of sun   of the sun
               Returning always,

And I laugh, silently.

Undersea Fragment in Colons

—Vicente Aleixandre—

Swordfish, I know you are tired: tired out with the sharpness of your face:
    Exhausted with the impossibility of ever
Piercing the shade: with feeling the tunnel-breathing streamline of your flesh
    Enter and depart   depart
              spirit-level after level of Death
        Tamped flat, and laid
Where there is no hillside grave.
        Take this as it settles, then: word
    That behind your incomparable weapon chokes and builds,
      Blocked and balanced in your sides
        Instinct with meridians: word: the x-mark of certain world-numbers
        Blood-brothering   rising blade-headed
To an element as basic as the water
              unraveling in layers from around you:
      Strata trapped and stitched
By your face like tapestry
         thinning   exploding
    The depth-imploded isinglass eye
           west of Greenwich and shocked
Into latitude   into the sea-birds' winged sea   tonnage of shifting silence now
      Freed to the unleashed Time
And timing of coordinates: all-solid light:

Pierceable sun   its flash-folded counterpart beneath
    By the billion: word: in one leap the layers,

    The slant ladder of soundlessness: word: world: sea:
     Flight partaking of tunnels   fins, of quills and airfoils:
      Word: unwitnessed numbers   nailed noon   enchanted three minutes
Of the sun's best effort of height   this space   time   this
     Hang-period   meridian passage:
          Sing.

Mexican Valley

—homage and invention, Octavio Paz—

The day works on
                    works out its transparent body.   With fire, the bodiless hammer,
Light knocks me flat.
                    Then lifts me.   Hooked on-
to the central flame-stone, I am nothing but a pause between
Two vibrations
                    of pressureless glow: Heaven
And trees.   Tlaloc help me
                    I am pure space:
One of the principle future-lost battlefields
Of light.   Through my body, I see my other bodies

Flocking and dancing   fighting each other
With solar joy.   Every stone leaps inward, while the sun tears out my eyes
And my Heaven-knifed, stone-drunken heart.
                    Yes,
But behind my gone sight is a spiral of wings.
                    Now   *now*
My winged eyes are fetched-back and singing: yes singing like buzzards
                    From the black-feathered crown-shifts of air
      Have always wished to be singing
                    over this valley.
And I lean over my song
      Within trees, God knows where,
                    in Mexico.
No matter what they say, it is not bad here.   No, it is good:
It is better than anything the astronomers can dream up
With their sweaty computers.   I've shaved my chest off to be
      Slowly-nearer and now without junk-hair
That is not really me   instantaneously nearer
      Soft universal power!   It is warm, it is maybe even a little
Too hot, but glorious, here at the center   all the center there is
Before history . . . I send you a searing Yes

138

From the thousand cross-glittering black-holes of obsidian:
I am like the *theory* of a blade
That closes rather than opens   *closes:*
That sends something back
Other than blood.   Among leaves, I have torn out the heart of the sun
The long-lost Mexican sun.

Low Voice, Out Loud

—Léon-Paul Fargue—

A good many times I've come down among you.
I've brought down my mountains, and washed them, just as a cloud would have done
But you   YOU   cannot even begin to guess the *space*
Of the great shadows that've just gone past us.
                              But, look:

I come out of you!
                I was your hands   your life-work
Your bleeding eyes   your red cubby-hole!   And that guitar:

To you, one touch of E minor is suicide!

I need you.
           I have lifted the anchor.
                       For the thousandth time
I have smelled your shoes.
               There I have done it, close to you and me:
I have lifted the anchor.
             Whoever loves well
Punishes well.   But don't go
Against my rhythm.
             It is by you that the man   in this case myself
Limits himself to being   his own being
A man: Identity blind, deaf
And indivisible!
             I am tired of existing
As an animal of intelligence—

Don't try to name what is nameless.

Nothing. Everything. Nothing.
                 Rest easy, love. It is best:
Let us go back into the immense and soft-handed, double

Fire-bringing ignorance.

Poem

—from the Finnish of Saima Harmaja—

O death, so dear to me,
Do you remember when someone loved you?

Let all our blood-kin come back, into
Your soft, embalmed half-shadow.

Look.   I'm making no gestures.
I like and don't like
Your diligent work.   I try not to pay attention.
Other troubles I can stand.   Not yours.

Free my soul
                    and open your blinding jail.

O my sweet, owned death,
Lift the used-up one,
The soul half-opened as a wound
                              and let him fly.

When

—Pierre Reverdy—

A prisoner in this space perpetually narrow
With my left-over hands left on my eyelids
With none of the words that reason can bring itself

To invent
        I play the hell-game
That dances on the horizon.   Space in darkness makes it better,

And it may be there are people passing through me—
There may even be a song
              of some kind

      The cloud fills itself full of hovering holes

      The needle loses itself
      In clothes-covered sharpness

      The thunder stops short—
A few more minutes
          I start to shake:
It's too late   too late ever to act   to act at all:

This is the thing as it will be.
All around, chains are gritting on each other
Like blackboard chalk   every tree
In the world is going to fall.

The window opens to summer.

A Saying of Farewell

—homage, Nordahl Grieg—

You've dressed yourself so white for it!   And you poise
As on the edge of an undersea cliff, for departure.
We two are the only ones who know that this lost instant
       Is not lost, but is the end
          Of life.

"It's as though we were dying, this calm twilight."
  No;   only you.   I hang on watch,
High up in Time.   Step off and fall as the wind rolls the earth

Over you like a wave.   I am left on duty with the heart
      Going out over everything, no sleep

       In sight   braced,   monster-eyed,
Outstaring the shaken powder of fatigue   mist—
      By your clothes and mine white-bled

Raging with discovery like a prow
      Into the oncoming Never.

Three Poems with Yevtushenko

I. I Dreamed I Already Loved You

I dreamed I already loved you.
I dreamed I already killed you.

But you rose again;   another form,
A girl on the little ball of the earth,
Naive simplicity, curve-necked
On that early canvas of Picasso,
And prayed to me with your ribs
"Love me," as though you said, "Don't push me off."

I'm that played out, grown-up acrobat,
Hunchbacked with senseless muscles,
Who knows that advice is a lie,
That sooner or later there's falling.

I'm too scared to say I love you
Because I'd be saying I'll kill you.

For in the depths of a face I can see through
I see the faces—can't count them—
Which, right on the spot, or maybe
Not right away, I tortured to death.

You're pale from the mortal balance. You say
"I know everything;   I was all of them.
I know you've already loved me.
I know you've already killed me.
But I won't spin the globe backwards
We're on: Love again, and then kill again."

Lord, you're young.   Stop your globe.
I'm tired of killing.   I'm not a damn thing but old.

You move the earth beneath your little feet,
You fall, "Love me."
It's only in those eyes—not similar—you say
"This time don't kill me."

II.   Assignation

No, no! Believe me!
                    I've come to the wrong place!
I've made a god-awful mistake!   Even the glass
In my hand's an accident
                    and so's the gauze glance
Of the woman who runs the joint.
                              "Let's dance, huh?
You're pale . . .
                    Didn't get enough sleep?"
And I feel like there's no place
To hide, but say, anyway, in a rush
"I'll go get dressed . . .
                    No, no . . . it's just
That I ended up out of bounds . . ."
And later, trailing me as I leave:
                              This is where booze gets
                                   you . . .
What do you mean, 'not here'? *Right* here! Right here every time!
You bug everybody, and you're so satisfied
With yourself about it.   Zhenichka,
You've got a problem."
                         I shove the frost of my hands
Down my pockets, and the streets around are snow,
Deep snow.   I dive into a cab.   Buddy, kick this thing!   Behind
                                        the Falcon
There's a room.   They're supposed to be waiting for me there.
She opens the door
                    but what the hell's wrong with her?
Why the crazy look?
                    "It's almost five o'clock.

You sure you couldn't come a little later?
Well, forget it.   Come on in.   Where else could you go now?"
Shall I explode

               with a laugh

                         or maybe with tears?
I tell you I was scribbling doggerel

                         but I got lost someplace.
I hide from the eyes.   Wavering I move backwards:
"No, no!   Believe me!   I've come to the wrong place!"
Once again the night

                   once again snow
and somebody's insolent song
and somebody's clean, pure laughter.
I could do with a cigarette.
In the blizzard Pushkin's demons flash past
And their contemptuous, bucktoothed grin
Scares me to death.

                And the kiosks
And the drugstores

               and the social security offices
Scare me just as much . . .

                 No, no!   Believe me!   I've ended up
In the wrong place again . . .

                 It's *horrible* to live
And even more horrible

               not to live . . .

                    Ach, this being homeless
Like the Wandering Jew . . . Lord!   Now I've gotten myself
Into the wrong century

               wrong epoch

                   geologic era

                         wrong number
The wrong place again

               I'm wrong

                   I've got it wrong . . .
I go, slouching my shoulders like I'd do
if I'd lost some bet,

and Ah, I know it . . . everybody knows it . . .
I can't pay off.

III.   Doing the Twist on Nails

When you throw your dancing shoes out, back over your shoulder,
And lose yourself, you find yourself twisting on the stage,
                              dancing,
                                 dancing,
                                    dancing—
let that pink boy whip you around—I can tell you:
Life doesn't dance this way—
                 That way dances death.
Thighs
          shoulders
                       breasts:
                                   they're all in it!
Inside you, dead drunk,
                           wheezes of air are dancing
Somebody else's ring
                       dances on your hand,
And your face by itself
                          doesn't dance at all
Flying, lifelessly, above all the body's life
Like a mask taken off your dead head.
And this stage—
                    is only one part of that cross
On which they once
                     crucified Jesus;
The nails shot through to the other side, and you began
To dance on them,
                     sticking out.
                                   And you dance
On the nails
                nails
On sandals red as rust
                        on the thorn-points of tears: Listen,
Because I once loved you, tiresomely, gloomily,

I also hammered the crooks of my nails

                                      into this page.

Ah, bestial, beastly music,

                         do you keep on getting stronger?

No one can see the blood

                      ooze from your foot-soles—

To wash the steps with clean water,

I'd rather you'd do it, Mary Magdalene,

                                   not Jesus.

I'll wash all their days, their yesterdays, not like a brother would

For a sister,

               but like a sister for a sister.

I'll kneel down and pick up your feet

And hold them quietly, and with kisses try to do something

About their wounds.

About the Author

James Dickey is a former night-fighter with more than 100 missions in World War II, an athlete, hunter, and woodsman, and author of a novel and screenplay, *Deliverance*. Now Poet in Residence and Carolina Professor at the University of South Carolina, he has taught at Rice University, Reed College, the University of Wisconsin, and the University of Florida. He has twice been appointed Poetry Consultant to the Library of Congress and in 1977 read a poem written in honor of President Carter at the Inaugural Concert Gala. He lives on Lake Katherine in Columbia, South Carolina.